Thoreau MacDonald's Notebooks

NOTEBOOKS

Thoreau MacDonald

Penumbra Press, 1980

Published by PENUMBRA PRESS, P.O. Box 340, Moonbeam, Ontario, POL 1VO.

Printed in Canada by The Porcupine's Quill, Inc., in July of 1980. The type is Stempel Garamond and the stock, Zephyr Antique Laid.

ISBN 0-920806-05-8 paper
0-920806-13-9 case

CONTENTS

Preface by Thoreau MacDonald
Foreword by Ray Nash
Note on the Text by John Flood

HESE PICTURES are attempts to show the Harmony & Design of Nature in a small space. All Nature is united and harmonious but in part there are often faults & discords, & as a picture is so limited it is best to eliminate the unnecessary & accentuate the essentials.

The artist tries to show the character, the everlasting nature within Nature which is in people as well & is what they really see or remember.

They represent more the spirit & feeling of the place & time than the outer appearance.

It is the idea or thought of a place or tree which is the reality to us & these are the artist's thoughts or concepts of Nature expressed in the limitations of paintings.

Thoreau MacDonald

HE WORK OF THOREAU MACDONALD in black and white line, which he has made very specially his own, has never been equalled, and will not be. Brought up in the midst of the Group of Seven, he of course did oil painting or water colour or used any convenient means of expression in any size. He made block prints, stencils, was a master of lettering and layout, designed magazine covers, bookplates, and worked in many styles. But his great work was in small size and in that most difficult of mediums, black and white pen and brush drawing. In a way that seems simple and effortless he could express heat or cold, weather and the seasons, the growth of each kind of tree, the flowing of water, the movement or stillness of animals, the flight of hawks or owls, and the work of the men who cultivated the land. Living and working outdoors himself, he understood the things tools make — houses and barns, fences and wagons. He drew these things with inner knowledge, and with even more sharp understanding he drew the wild animals watching the work of men from a little distance. Thoreau MacDonald is himself the expressionless man sawing his winter wood. He is even more the sharp-eyed fox watching at a distance along the edge of a field. The drawings are small windows through which we see, briefly stated, things never expressed in words about the condition of man in the world, and of the wild creatures who live their own life alongside him.

Ray Nash

HE MAKING OF THIS BOOK is owing to the inspiration of the man who is its author and subject. Thoreau Mac-Donald, heralded for over fifty years as a master of lettering, book design, and line drawing, here offers a glimpse of the development of his craft. This is not an autobiography, for in many ways Thoreau dislikes that genre of writing. Yet a great deal about his personality is revealed, so much so that we see him as the ideal exponent of a lifestyle whose credo, 'Ain't Nature Grand,' is genuine.

Thoreau MacDonald's closeness to nature is evident in his subjects: landscapes, animals in their natural habitat, and plain and simple folk on the farm or in the bush. At one time he was himself a small farmer and perhaps was happiest when maneuvering a tractor or working with his hands; his artwork convincingly projects this harmony. Somewhat reclusive, perhaps even ascetic, he practises a form of humanism that is patterned after his namesake. Reducing the complications of living to their simplest forms also demonstrates another Thoreauvian maxim, one taught by his father: 'Form Follows Function.'

Thus, if some of Thoreau's illustrations appear simple it is because the function which they serve is clearly dictated by their suggestive value. The pine and spruce trees, for example, are common subjects whose form is representative of reality rather than an exact copy. While the simplicity of design is sometimes quite detailed — as in illustrations of loons or horses — it is rarely sacrificed for the sake of a meticulously created replica. In making drawings, Thoreau exploits their reductive quality, their ability to suggest recognizable reality or parts thereof. Their simple and lyrical tone evokes a complementary mood in the viewer.

In the case of book illustration, his technique is to read the manuscript thoroughly and to illustrate those passages which encapsulate the inner life of the author's subject matter. He calls the

preliminary drawings 'notes' and from them he makes his final line drawings. The notes are quick and rough pencil sketches from various points of view. After making several of them and selecting the best ones as models, he duplicates them by blackening their reverse sides with pencil, places them on a clean sheet of paper, and heavily traces their outline. He then adds details to the new outline on the second sheet.

The notes in this volume are important because they are, for the most part, previously unpublished. Of the more than 100 reproduced here, our aim has been to provide examples representative of Thoreau's best work throughout his career. In addition, all of Thoreau's writing – with one exception – is previously unpublished.

The first two chapters consist of diaries which Thoreau has kept from an early age; he refers to them as 'notebooks.' Chapter I is a facsimile reproduction of his 1912 summer diary and Chapter II is a selection of entries from notebooks between 1931 and 1976. Many of the citations in this chapter are also to be found on the walls of the back entrance to Thoreau's house in Thornhill. As unusual events unfolded he would describe them and occasionally speculate on their uncommonness.

Chapter III reveals Thoreau's natural story-telling ability; we might conjecture that if he had not become an artist (a word whose applicability he doubts), he conceivably could have become a writer. 'Talks with a Hunter' is reprinted from its original (and long out of print) Woodchuck Press publication and is a fine example of Thoreau's wit and humour.

Chapters IV to VIII provide an interesting blend of shoptalk and personal bits of information. They consist of letters to Doris Heustis Mills, Carl Schaefer, Ray Nash, Lorne Pierce, and Norman Kent in which Thoreau is always a gentleman, always a friend. While the dates of most letters are known, those in brackets [ ] represent editorial intrusions to indicate either presumed dates or, when a question mark [?] is included, that not even presumed dates can be established.

And finally, the chapter on Maria Chapdelaine is a selection of notes which, when compared with that book's ink drawings, allow for a new dimension of analysis. We can see how Thoreau would sometimes alter the composition when doing the ink drawing — in the note for 'Grace Before Meals' the cat cuddles Chapdelaine's boots and the boy stands devoutly on both feet, whereas in the ink drawing both the cat and the boy's right leg are resting on the bench; and in 'Edwidge Légaré Shaving' the cat's position is sedate in the note and active (like Légaré, he too is grooming himself) in the ink drawing. In both cases the *carpe diem* stillness of the note develops in time and place.

In compiling the material for this book I am indebted to many people for their invaluable assistance. I am grateful to Doris Heustis Speirs and Ray Nash for providing access to their collections of letters and drawings by Thoreau MacDonald, and to the Thomas Fisher Rare Book Library, Toronto; the Douglas Library, Queen's University, Kingston; the National Library of Canada, Ottawa; Redpath Library, McGill University, Montréal; Syracuse University Library, Syracuse; the National Gallery of Canada, Ottawa; the Art Gallery of Ontario, Toronto; Dartmouth College, Hanover, for access to their archival holdings. And thanks also to the many people with whom I corresponded. To Carl Schaefer, a

NOTE ON THE TEXT

great friend of Thoreau's, can be attributed a motivation and encouragement that helped this book to come alive; I thank him for that. And I am most grateful to Thoreau MacDonald whose guidance and understanding are warmly appreciated.

Acknowledgements are also owing to Macmillan of Canada, McClelland and Stewart, Ryerson Press, Farrar and Rinehart, and the Woodchuck Press; to *Trinity University Review, Acta Victoriana, Print,* and the *Canadian Forum;* to the McMichael Canadian Collection and to the Stinehour Press.

John Flood

CHAPTER I

Diary of 1912 in Facsimile

July 12 th   1912

Dad and I went
to the other end of
the island this morning
Coming back we saw
a wood-chuck→ (a fisher).
We fished some I
caught three and Dad
caught five but he
only kept two
Mine were the biggest
one of them was
dragon-flies are almost
as good as cracker-
jacks

Fisher

I made a motor boat
today it works pretty
good

July 13 th
   It was awfully windy
today the waves were
as high as the ceiling
When we were having
our dinner a squall
came. It rained like
everything and everything
blew around Dad had
to run out and put
an extra rope and

July 15th

It was raining like
everything today
and hailing too
so we didnt do anything
Jay fell in and had
to swim to shore
Dad helped me to
fix a rudder on my
boat tonight

July 16th.

Dad went down to
go home today

MacCallum's turtle isn't
as big as the one over
here

The Trader came
today and we went
out to it and got
some stuff

We went up Monument
Channel this afternoon

I made a raft but
it wouldn't hold me

July 17th

We went down to go
Home this morning.
We saw three young
crows on a rock
waiting for their mother
to bring them something
to eat I guess.
On the way back we
saw a little mud turtle
and tried to scoop him
up but we couldn't.
We saw a big fish
laying eggs.

July 18th.

I caught a lot of Minno
today but I let them
go again you can
see right through them
in some places they look
like this ⊂——◁ I found
a different kind of crab
claw ⊂◼ ⊂◼ the first
one is the ordinary
kind and the next is the
kind I found

July 19th

We saw a mink
today I was
right up close to him
We saw a lune too
he came right up
close and didn't see
us
There was a woodpecker
up in a pine on the
burnt island its the
first one I've seen
up here
I let the snapper go
today I guess he was
glad to get away

July 20th
I caught 5 snails today
and put them in a jar
their faces look like
cows they are
water snails
The Trader came today

July 21 st
I got a little dead
fish today and fed
him to the mud turtle
he ate him.
he was just like a
big fish only little
I can row pretty
well now
I got a lot of little
snail shells I broke
one open and it looks
like this

July 22 nd.

I saw a crane today
over round the burnt
island
We rowed in around
the little channelbo at
the other end of the
island I got two snail
shells and the inside
of one it looks like
a corkscrew ▲

July 23rd.

We saw the old duck
today with her young
ones she's only got four
now, I saw two other
ducks too

I got some of the little
round kind of snails
they can go faster than
the others

Mother saw a woodchuck
but I didn't though

July 24th.

We went and got
some huckleberries
today some ar not quite
ripe yet but we got
all ripe ones
We rowed over to
Macallums tonight and
Bert gave us a tow
back

July 25 th

We went down to go
Home this morning
and saw the Waubic
come in.

I caught two minnows
today they're growing
quite a bit

There were two big
fish under the house
boat tonight I think
they were suckers

I saw a crane
in the lily pond
today

July 26th.

W saw a ^{heron} crane right
close in the lily-pond
I saw it through the
glasses

I know where a crab
lives under a rock he has
a little gravel walk out at
the front I saw him
come out twice

We killed a snake three
feet long up where the tent
was Mother like to sit there.
. I saw two cranes
fly out of the lily pond

July 27 th.

We went over to an island near the gorklome channel today and it was so windy coming back we could hardly get across

I saw a lot of young ducks there were about sixteen when they get going they make quite a swell.

July 28th:

Dad went to Indian
Harbour in MacAllum's
launch today
When we were getting
the supper about thirty
ducks came around
the corner they weren't
scared a bit there
was a big one leading
them and a big white one
at the back
I saw a crane tonight

July 2 9 nth.

We rowed a little way.
up the island and landed
Tony had a woochuck.
down a hole
I found a little blue
flower call the blue
toad flax
I found a different
kind of water snail
He'd been on a log when
the water was high and
it went down and left
him dry 🐚 he was a
sort of greenish gold
colour I put him back

July 31st.

We saw a gull with a
dead fish in the lily-pond
eating the fish. there
were a lot of crows
watching. Then a crane
came and chased the
gull away and started
to eat the fish

We went a chased them
off and brought the
fish nearer the gull
came and ate him all

We rowed down to go Home
and saw the Waubic
come in

August 1st.
We killed a fox snake
four feet long and brought
him home   We caught
two black bass

August second
We rowed up to the goddame
channell and lost our
troll an the way over
We went out to the supply
boat too
I saw the cranes flying
over its raining tonight
we didnt do much today

_____

Agust 3rd.
We went upto Sandy
grays falls where Sandy
gray was drowned
We saw some deer
tracks and four or five
wolf tracks
We had to portage
twice. We saw a
dead deer and I found
an old pury and Dad
found an old ax
The Doctor caught a
big pike and Bert
caught a pike and a
pickerel they were
all about two feet
long

August 4 th

We didn't do hardly
anything today
but I saw a gull
sitting on the water
right outside
the houseboat

august 5 th.

Nothing happened today
only I saw three cranes
and a turtle

CHAPTER II

Notes Around Home, 1931-1976

(These fragments come from notebooks recording weather, sightings of aurora, birds & animals or anything of interest, mostly ordinary, everyday events.)

OCTOBER 26, 1931: Today going west from Steeles Corners met an old man repairing his laneway with a load of stones he had drawn there on his stoneboat. His horse was old & furry & they were escorted by a fine, strong collie. In the distance a black Jersey cow grazed in the ditch. She was tied to the telephone pole. The wind blew cold across that high, open piece of country but at the edge of the long grass four gray & white cats were sitting in the sun &

watching the work. When I returned the old man had finished & was just turning his horse out into the stubble while the dog barked & leaped around before them. A very fine dog.

AN OLD SPOON. This old spoon, worn out of true & the plating almost gone, belonged to Grandmother, Susan Prior Lavis. The interesting part is that she bought it with her first money earned at the Woods' store, an old stone house at Taylor's Corners, east of Oakwood.

SEPTEMBER 27, 1935: Brought several roots of Wild Aster from Tutt's pasture. Two trips in the rain. The start of all our hundreds of plants.

SEPTEMBER 28, 1935: Took the wire fence off maples on west line. Someone had tacked the wire to the trees & it's grown in. Hacksawed live wires off close to the bark & hope it will cover them. All vanished eventually.

They say cut wood for construction in October. Walter says always cut in full moon.

Cleaned out the trunk of old snow tree S.E. of house. Several ants, nests & a mouse nest of paper etc. A slim light gray mouse rushed distracted up the tree. Entire trunk gone but a sound semi-circular shell.

OCTOBER 15, 1935: Tonight visited the men working on F.B.H. house on the 3rd of Markham. I see their fire through the bush & can hear Frenchy & Frank (Polish) talking about riding the freights on Canadian transcontinental trips. Walter is carving a violin neck with a home made knife like. . . .

He tells of some bad cases of blood poisoning & the cure. A poultice of rolled oats boiled in milk & kept on hot. This from an old Indian up near Windsor who saved a man's arm so after doctors wanted to amputate. Returning by moonlight I heard the ghosts under the John St. bridge. Also met 2 skunks on the walk in front of United Church. They ran to & fro before me & in front of a passing car which slowed up. Left them under the church steps.

OCTOBER 26, 1935: One of the 3 largest elms cut. It had developed a lean. Circ. 12′4″ & 150 to 200 rings.

JANUARY, 1936: Talking with Walter about windmills. The pegs or teeth in the big wooden gears were made of wild apple or hard maple.

MARCH 27, 1936: Snow nearly gone. A very cold, steady winter & great damage by mice. A fence line tree 12″ dia. completely stripped for a foot above ground. A queer idea of Nature's to sacrifice a production that takes a hundred years to grow just to feed a few wretched mice. Mama knows best.

APRIL 19, 1936: Talking with W. about axes, he tells of Russian axemen & their skill. Much work on log buildings done without other tools. Even window frames he says. Going home in the evenings they toss their axes high in the air & as they descended whirling, catch them by the handle. They could lay their hand on a block with fingers spread & bring the hatchet down full force between the fingers in quick succession. W. says in threshing with a flail the sheaves are laid in pairs, head to head with hands cut. Hot work even in midwinter.

JUNE 12, 1936: At Alf Wright's to see if he wants hay. He has his homemade shingles on the house now. 'Good for 50 years. Yes I froed them out 4 to the inch thick.' Too much crossgrain in sawn shingles. He could cradle 6 acres a day & he could do an acre an hour. Had a wonderful cradle, a man named Sylvester made the frame and the blade would go around a 10 acre field without sharpening. It measured 5′. so he cut a 10′. swath & 'she went through the grain faster than I could follow, a sweet cutting blade.' Jonathon Baker, father of Jesse, would walk 5 miles to pay you 3¢, Alf says.

JUNE 30, 1936: Tomorrow is the first of July. Temp. tonight 46°. At

Alf's the other night found him sawing up stumps with his circular saw. Scary to see the shaky, old man (83) pushing the stumps into the howling saw.

JULY 13, 1936: 25 days since rain & for 5 days temperature reached 105°. in the shade.

OCTOBER 30, 1937: A very clear night with many shooting stars. 8 PM hear geese honking. Many flocks passing at once. They continue for 3 hours & sound very fine in the clear starry sky with many meteors.

SEPTEMBER, 1938: An early frost; frequent frosts. Two sounds of the autumn night — thump of falling apples & chirps of migrating birds.

OCTOBER 2, 1938: Sunday. Ed had bought 10 sheep who follow an old sow around the field. M. tells us how one of the hens lost all its feathers. 'It got sunburned & when the first cold nights came didn't it get left outside & die.' They were scalding a pig at the time and E. thought to boil the hen for Lindy (a dog) so when she seemed done he forked her out & laid her on the ground to cool & that old Paddy dog of Snider's came & carried it off home. So Lindy lost his chicken dinner after all.

OCTOBER 30, 1938: Sunday. Fine & warm. Walked through Carreville to the 3rd, south & home past Baker's & through Ed's. In the Carreville swamp met an old Tomcat catching grasshoppers. He yodeled to me from the sedge & finally came out & walked with me for a long way. Nicer country at the corner of Carreville Rd. & the 3rd concession. A dry ditch in the fields enters a grove of cedar & comes out a small stream. Found a small bronze sleighbell embedded in the road & managed to dig it out. The ringer rusted away but bronze good as new. Few hawks this fall.

NOVEMBER, 1938: This month at last wonderfully warm.

NOVEMBER 24, 1938: First snow. Last week a warm spring like rain. Toads came out & many killed on highway.

MARCH 3, 1939: Deep snow & bearing crust. A ringed moon at 8:30. The ring not a circle but a long ellipse. Moon almost overhead. New to me.

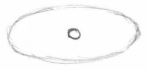

EASTER, 1939: To Orangeville. Much snow in woods & valleys. Streams swollen & rushing green over limestone rocks & through ice snow. The big spring runs exactly as in summer, no more, no less. Herons overhead. An old man ploughing the hard drifts with a field plough. His boys then shovel the loosened snow off the road.

JUNE 11, 1939: The Dresden Meteor. Early evening. Still sunlight. Standing in the door of Ed's pumphouse, he working on the engine inside; all at once the whole interior lighted up & I saw my shadow on the wall opposite. We swung 'round & saw an immense meteor falling down the s.w. sky making a trail of light against the sunset. Julia B. saw it from Go Home Bay. A Gov't astronomer visited us & by taking an angle from our two viewpoints they located it near Dresden, Ontario. (See meteor book, 'Out of the Sky.')

JULY, 1939: Fireblight kills nearly all our pear trees.

AUGUST, 1940: Helping J. Pearson drawing hay from Cemetery land. As we came near the gate in the wagon he announced cheerfully, 'We're going right over old Jimmy Wells.'

DECEMBER 11, 1940: A mild spell after sub zero. Heavy snow keeps the ground from freezing & it's free from frost with worms near the surface. Many mice & cats unable to do much owing to the snow. Heard different owl calls. A landmark. Finding Blue Cohosh in Orangeville maple bush. Never saw it before. Ed says they saw a fox pass the barnyard chased by two dogs. 2nd I've heard of lately & the start of a brief increase in their numbers.

FEBRUARY, 1941: Many foxes seen & some reported shot. E.S. says

8 in this area. One man saw one asleep on a stump all day long while he ploughed nearby with a tractor.

AUGUST 1, 1941: Picking off tomato worms with Ed. He says, 'Man I hate these things. I could kill one end and watch the other suffer.' Several deer seen here.

THANKSGIVING, 1941: Saw a beautiful brown marsh hawk playing with a crow over J. Reaman's fields. The hawk never seems to try to escape but evades the crow with quick turns & rolls. Sometimes turns on her back & presents her claws. Autumn coloured woods beyond.

OCTOBER 26, 1941: At Orangeville. Saw a young Red Tail standing upright in a field & close to the road. Seems to be standing over his prey. Head & chest white, brown body spotted & striped back. A Goshawk flies overhead. In woods a large brown, hawklike owl. Dark round head & ears, maybe longeared owl. Flies swiftly away. Brown beneath.

FEBRUARY 28, 1942: Poor old Specks, our best cat, died. I heard a slight sound at 1 AM & found him dead without a struggle or any sign of sickness. 5 years old, a fine, strong cat. His brother Stripey came in & rushed outdoors distracted.

MARCH 15, 1942: To Baker's maple bush. No buckets out yet. Cloudy but lively weather. Gulls overhead, thousands of goldfinches. Many skunk tracks on roads. A pheasant leaps up & strikes fence wire.

MARCH 26, 1942: Geese going over at sunset. On Sunday walking to Baker's (sap buckets out) I thought of the old names around here. Walked w. from Langstaffe's corners & down Bingo Hill past Beggar's Lane & Slabtown where the remains of the sawmill dam still show. From Bingo Hill look N.W. to Mt Misery & Honeypot. Turn south at Jesse's Bush & go through Bear Trap Hollow & past Cooper's Slash.

MARCH 29, 1942: At the sugar camp. A. is cutting wood for next year. Needs 15 cords per season. Rode around with Mr B. & nearly filled 2 barrels. He says sap stops running before a storm. At some trees not a drop, others the buckets overflow. They've made 100 gal. so far & expect 200. First frogs heard.

APRIL, 1942: The Skunk Trapper. Being bothered with skunks under the porch (they fight) I remembered a famous skunk expert in Richvale & after hunting for some time was directed to his home by 2 little girls, a homemade hovel west of the village. A little lamp burning showed the tiny interior crowded with a range & table.

47

Heard sawing & voices at back & found him & his mother building a wee bit of hay shed (she said). Sure he'd clean them out, smoke 'em out. Kits don't come till June he says.

A fine collie was jumping up on me & showing off all his tricks. A little stream runs almost under their shack & into the swamp beyond. Returning see a fine Aurora.

AUGUST, 1942: Saw for first time Black Crowned Night Herons, 3 at J. Reaman's Creek. Helped J.P. bag up oats & asked if he'd sell them to D. 'That hound! He's another J.S. McLean. He's got 2 children & if they turn out like him, God help this world.'

OCTOBER, 1942: Stayed overnight by Nottawasaga Creek. Too cold to sleep well so listened all night to the rapids & hooting of two Horned Owls. The woods wild & ancient with shaggy spruce & rocks & bright jays flitting around. Note inaccuracy in Marsh Hawk drawings. Wings shorter & rounded. They are tearing down Hugh Hewson's old log house. Some spaces between windows & doors filled in with masonry. Mixed materials.

OCTOBER, 1942: E. says, 'A funny thing happened last night. One of them little pigs in there stretched out flat, like dead. I picked him up & there seemed no life, just gave a few twitches. I thought the old sow stepped on him; laid him out on a manure pile. He jumped up & ran inside, just asleep all the time.' John complains of plough wearing out. E. says 'You're like Jim Acey's man, he broke the plough & when he told the old man Jim says, "Now that's funny, I've used that plough for 50 years & it never broke till now".'

E. told about Peter Huff, a German who lived on Yonge St. in the old Horan house. His cow was a great one for opening gates so Peter had various devices to keep her penned up. E's father & Mattie Pegg got an old cow's foot from the slaugher house & made tracks all over Peter's garden, puzzling him very much how the cow opened & closed the gate.

Told about Ed Langstaffe after thrashing at Randal Page's. It got dark & Ed pretended he was afraid to go home through the swamp & asked an Englishman to go with him. Ed led him into the thickest part of the bush then said he was OK now & left him. The poor Englishman never got out until morning.

Also how someone dug out two woodchucks at Ed Mellon's over on the 2nd of Markham. Ed told him as long as he carried them by the tails they couldn't move so the greenie started for home carrying the poor chucks. All went well till his arms tired & the chucks came nearer his legs & finally took hold with their big teeth. You could hear him yell 80 rods off.

E's old pigs have a little door to their pen & a curtain to keep out the cold. He throws down a couple forkfulls of straw & before long they carry it all inside & make their beds. He never needs to put it in for them.

Better Than Nothing. The fox hid under the harrow from the rain. 'Not all the drops will fall on me anyhow' (Russia). 'It's all settled,' as the hen said when she lit on the water (Norway).

DECEMBER 10, 1942: The little Siskins seem able to fly straight up & down. A Canadian poets says, 'Cow byre' & spoils his whole poem for me. I wish they would use such Ontario words as Fence Corner, Cedar Swamp, Maple Bush, Chore-time, Forenoon, Driving Shed, Stoneboat.

DECEMBER 20, 1942: Cold. At 7 PM our 3 thermometers stood at 22, 30 & 34: below 0.

FEBRUARY, 1943: E. says as he cleans the cow stable, 'My uncle Tom always said, "Don't let the manure gather around the door. Take 5 steps & then throw it far as you can".'

FEBRUARY, 1943: 29° below the other day now a soft springlike night. Rabbit in the moonlight under the window. Just as 30 years ago.

APRIL 17, 1943: To Baker's for syrup & carry home a 15 lb can 4 miles. A fine, bright & cool day with snow going off. Mr. B. says sap is running again after none all week. He repeats that you never can tell when it will run. Returning, see Sparrow hawk, fox tracks & a Whiskey jack.

JUNE 20, 1943: Sunday. Two hares are fighting & playing in the road. Stand erect & make their paws fly like boxers. Invited in to

A Letter from Home

FROM A SOLDIER OF 1914–18 TO A SOLDIER OF 1939–19?

Mr John Page's, a ½ mile walk up his lane. The bricks of the house made & fired on the farm 75 years ago. A fine solid house & neat yard. Told how Jim Pearson bought pigs from him for 40 years. One morning just at daybreak Jim arrived for a load. Then Mr P. noticed 3 hens on the axle of the wagon. They had been roosting there & rode out the 2½ miles from home.

SEPTEMBER, 1943: A Dream of walking to the village & feeling sad over trees being cut, etc. Got as far as Boyles & thought things looked strange & great changes going on. There was a board shelter over the sidewalk such as they build when tearing down houses. I passed through this & came out in a strange town never seen before. Had a short struggle to return or adjust myself & then realized I must have died on the road & was in another world. It was an old style Ontario country town & lots of country people were walking around. I felt lost but decided to walk west, my favourite way, so asked a young man, 'Which is North?' He pointed & I started westward thinking how upset my folks would be. A very queer feeling. It seemed a cold, cloudy fall day & the roads were muddy. Picket fences, weigh scales, hitching posts & everything old style.

This morning saw a skunk lying by the sidewalk & smelling very strong. I think I'll have to bury him but returning later met 3 small boys who are loading him in a little wheelbarrow. They say they are going to take him home to show their folks.

DECEMBER 7, 1943: Lots of mild, still weather. As Ed was unhitching from the plough he said, 'I mind when Tom Lane had that place where Watson is; we used to climb the fence & change the rack of his plough. Then in the morning going to school we heard him shouting, "Haw, Haw," and the old plough would be scooting off to one side. Well, jokes like that aren't bad but I never did hold with breaking things like the kids do nowadays.' I told him how one of the old Pearson brothers who are retiring to the village was heard talking to his cat in the barn, 'Well kit, did you know you're going to move?'

APRIL 24, 1944: To Orangeville in mist & rain. How wild there comparatively. The clear rushing Nottawasaga water, rocks & snowy spruce, alders, snow white pussy willows. The mist rolls up like smoke over the cedar swamp. Got stuck coming out & had to borrow a team from 2 very nice boys who refused any pay.

MAY, 1944: Talking to Ed in the Granary. He told how one of the Lanes driving his new car through the back of the driving shed & hollering, 'Whoa, Whoa, blast you.' While we talked Ed's old 3-legged cat & one of her daughters came in & sat on the granary stairs, just level with our shoulders. When E. speaks they look in his face. When I say something they turn their heads & look from one to the other with serious attention. Later I saw Ed behind the big elm in the lane trying for a shot at crows. Nip crouches waiting the report & the old cat at Ed's side. She looks around on the alert for game. She knows what the gun means.

OCTOBER, 1944: A spell of cool, cloudy weather after the equinox. Grand skies of heavy clouds moving & changing without wind. Sunday. About 2 months ago we saw a kitten hunting by the road near Reaman's creek. Thinking she might get shot at we coaxed her up & J.B. carried her to R's house. Yest. Passing the same place we hear a sudden meow & out she comes & insists on being picked up. So confident are they.

NOVEMBER, 1944: A feature of this fall is the amount of still, cloudy weather, especially nights, perfect stillness.

JANUARY, 1945: Ed's old cat, age 13, has been failing & died today. Ed had been nursing her along for over a year. At evenings I heard the snap of his .22 when he was getting her a sparrow to keep her strength up.

FEBRUARY, 1945: Average of 6 measures of snow 22 ⅓″.

MARCH, 1945: Very early Spring. March 15 temp. at 4 PM 70°. Seeding well along. Grass ready to cut. Saw a fox glide up the hillside like a cloud shadow. Jim complains of a barking dog. 'Yap, yap, all day. He barks at the leaves on the trees.'

NOVEMBER 3, 1945: At Walter Watt's sale. While the team was driven up & down the dog runs alongside rolling up his eyes at the horses & people. W's driver, a powerful, long-legged horse, brought $21.00, buggy 2.00, cutter 50¢. An old bay horse with a swollen leg watches over the pasture fence. E. is selling out too but he bought a tub of old bolts, etc.

FEBRUARY 14, 1946: 4:30 AM. Wind strikes after rain & reaches 72 mph. Bar. goes to 28.4-.

FEBRUARY 25, 1946: 11″ of snow quietly fell. It has a yellow tinge & mixed with very fine dust maybe from western US dust storms or the Mexican volcano.

APRIL 2, 1946: When Nip rushed into the yard to drive back the pigs one of the cats scampered out to see the excitement. A little heifer took after the cat & while capering around slipped & fell with a thump. She got up looking embarrassed while the cat watched calmly from the rails.

APRIL 20, 1946: Puss died of wounds in mouth, cause unknown. One of our best cats & a great loss. It's sad when they think you will help them. A great loss.

MAY 28, 1946: Helping J.P. plant spuds. A fine evening light on barn & lilacs. Team, barns, & light seem of the past. Soon there'll be no trace of that quiet old way of life, only cars, trucks, & jets. Jim says our front line of maples was planted by Johnson Wilson & when Jim came to Thornhill 70 years ago they were stout, young trees. Present house built about 1910.

AUGUST 11, 1946: First days of fall . . . Sun Rays through clouds (Eyes of God). One says a sure sign of 10 days of good weather. Lasts 5 days then showers.

SEPTEMBER 5, 1946: Big migration of night hawks. Flitting everywhere, filling the sky (Never see them now '70).

SEPTEMBER 16, 17, & 18, 1946: Hot weather. Aurora every night.

SEPTEMBER 25, 1946: 2 AM Barometer falls to 28.1 Gale moderates 10 PM.

THANKSGIVING, 1946: Got a load of manure from Pearsons. I asked how the old bay horse was. 'Oh he's getting kind of childish like me I guess.' Mild rainy fall but J. expects a hard winter. 'Such a heavy coat of leaves.' This is the end of our section as real country. Fields & fences I've known for 30 years are invaded & I never go where I used to go. On my way to the field I heard J.P. fixing the ladders on the rack & saying, 'Well, are you going to help us?' When I asked who he had been talking to he says, 'Just a little gray bird came & sat on the rack.'

MARCH 23, 1947: First warm day & floods. Last week expected to find Bakers in the sugar bush but been too cold they say. Must be melting in the shade. Henry Winger says, 'Now boys, no use to tap while you have to wear mitts.'

AUGUST 20, 1947: First cool day after long hot spell. 3 nights of Aurora. Weather abnormal, not recognizable.

OCTOBER 8, 1947: Fixing the roof on Jim's stable, heard the clanging of geese & a big v passes over to S.E.

MARCH, 1948: Lots of cold weather. Going into the stable with Jim he says, 'Now I've come over to the barn without a license.' I couldn't understand until he explained he wanted an old car license plate to tack over a hole in the floor.

JUNE 19, 1948: Started haying on N.W. field. Getting Jim's wagon gear ready, putting in long reach, greasing wheels. Talked of wagon builders, Trench's works, Richmond Hill, Speight Bain, Adams, George Ley, Teston. Jim said, 'Old W. Robinson was out in his garden today. But he strained his eyes looking for a weed & had to go in.'

JULY 20, 1948: Finished alfalfa. Very hot but escaped rain, only 6 loads.

JANUARY 18 & 19, 1949: 4 AM Wind increased. Clouds broke & rushed across moon. Wind reached 82 mph.

JANUARY, 1949: Cutting & splitting some big choke cherry trees that died suddenly last year. Biggest I've seen, 7″ dia. Heavy & hard wood.

JANUARY 3, 1950: Poor kit died after 3 days illness. Sickness & death of animals is a painful thing in life. Memories of their futile appeals & unavailing reliance on me. A lively, humorous, clever & affectionate kitten.

MARCH, 1950: Sawing a big hickory blown down in storm. Saved out some for handles. Ed tells of one old hen who eats eggs. He went in the coop with a flashlight & saw an egg on the floor. But this old hen saw it too though he thought her asleep on the perch. She hopped down like a flash & nabbed it. B.H. when he got drunk always climbed a tree. He was the one who never set nor sharpened his saw but would go to the bush with his old pipe upside down & saw all day on one log & one cut. He'd stand over the stove warming his hand & absently swaying then put them to the hot stove & yell, 'Lord how I suffer.'

APRIL 12, 1950: Went to Baker's sugar bush. Very cold with grand clouds & snow flurries. A. showed me his father's grave, a small semi-circular stone, white & new at the end of a row of gray & old mossy ones. All exactly alike. Showed me his new pipeline in the woods with covered & screened funnels at intervals. We visited some of the best trees, one tapped every spring since 1870. At his sawmill he has been cutting some pines that are gradually dying. Why? The pine era seems over here. (See H.D.T. *Succession of Forest Trees.*) A. plans to set out 5000 trees this spring. He says he always wants to be learning. (80% of these young trees were later destroyed by mice.) A.B. is a wonderfully capable & farsighted character. Has a phone in the sugar camp. Burning waste cork & rubber to save wood. They need 25 cords each spring. When we drove in, the little girls ran to open the gate, then stood around silently smiling. A. says he has tried to persuade neighbours to buy farms & prevent subdivision. Unsuccessful. He bought J. Reaman's old stump fence for fuel, but Edna didn't want the old stumps burnt so he made them into a fence again, west of the bush. 'She likes a stump fence.'

APRIL 20, 1950: Gray & cold, snow-flurries, clear air & dark intense colours of distant fields, hills & woods seen from Ed's high ridge. We were burning brush & stumps. After eating I offered to help wash dishes but E. says, 'I'll do them tonight when I'm alone & talking to myself & get up an argument.'

SEPTEMBER 23, 1950: Yellowish dust coloured clouds overspread the sky except N & N.E. Dark blue black in s.w. Overhead fine ripples like tide marks. The sun now & then shows as a violet blue disc. Never saw such a thing before. Attributed to fires in Alberta.

MAY, 1952: L. Hatfield mourning the loss of his hammer. 'Why I loved that old hammer.' He says, 'I used to have a lovely stoneboat out at the farm.'

SEPTEMBER 2, 1952: Very wonderful sunset. Fiery clouds flying from N.W. Whole sky a mass of fiery smoke, more like the world's end than any I ever saw. (May 31, 1962 the same.)

OCTOBER, 1952: Last summer Ed sold out & now the last of the near farmland has gone. The long front lane where we found the bits of blue glass. The short cut through the orchard & down the slope to the swamp. The back lane to the high fields westward. Ed's old cat, too old to scratch, lingered on at the old place for many weeks, then all at once appeared at his new house & settled there. The houses ½ mile apart on a busy highway. A striking variation in cat nature. Nip, the dog, brought her, his old friend.

DECEMBER 6, 1952: Helped Jim burn an old wagon for scrap. In these advanced times horses are killed for mink & the wagons burned so the iron can go for scrap. Advancing civilization. Stamped in the iron was GEORGE LEY. J. says came from Teston. I saved this.

FEBRUARY, 1953: Baker's sap buckets out. Started February 25, earliest ever. Previous early date March 5. A. is installing oil burner in sugar house, his own design. Has 3600 gal. of oil in underground tank. Also a portable drill for tapping. Everything modern but the trees. Doubt the syrup will taste as good. Cold, with fine clouds & gleams on snowy Oak Ridges.

MARCH 24, 1953: At sugar camp, a very, very poor run. Saw several bitting seedling pines under maples & in Bear Trap one growing in a pine stump. (See H.D.T. *Succession of Forest Trees.*)

MARCH 24, 1953: Talked with Ed & McN. re. Swamp whiskey & moonshining. An old moonshiner by the Saugeen R. told him, 'This is a great life. When I'm out at the still all night, stars & big trees all 'round, I tell you a man's got to know there's a God.'

MARCH 25, 1954: Poor old black puss, Georgie, died. 17 yrs. old. Mildest & most gentle of all. Never chased birds who hopped & pecked all 'round her. Greatly missed.

MARCH 31, 1954: A good run so far but too cold now. 2 black ducks rise from the creek & 2 duck hawks play & scream above. Dark cattle on snowy speckled hillside look like Muskox.

AUGUST, 1954: H. Neal showed me a pine 42″ wide (measured it myself) Came from a barn near R.R. south of Steele's (Buchanan?)

FEBRUARY, 1955: To Isaac Baker's for mitts. He said he studied phrenology once & demonstrated some points on his helper. Fine still winter day the shop sunny & all in order. Cheerful view from his bench to the western hardwood bush. Returning met A. & Paul with 4 men clearing up fallen timber & saving any fit for saw logs. He's proud of a new sleigh made of single bob, the front end rests on the tractor hitch . . . makes short easy turns.

FEBRUARY, 1956: Talked with Ed about old Ev. Dunn who often wore fur cap & mitts in summer. Ed told of another eccentric who long ago sold curry combs & brushes near the market. Always wore a long heavy coat & whispered, 'Any curry combs? Brushes?' even though no one was near. Ed says that whispered question haunts him still. A Dream: I saw a great expanse of grass sloping to the N. & a straight grassy track leading to the s. horizon. Two little old frame houses opposite each other by the road. One on left an open shed with some old wooden implements. I was creeping southward up the slope with awful weariness & effort. Sun clear from the w. about 4 PM. Sometimes pulled myself along by the grass as often happens in dreams.

DECEMBER, 1956: Ed told about Joe Feeney who liked a drink. One Sunday there were visitors at the farm. They were sitting on the porch when someone took a faintish spell & Mrs S. brought some brandy. Soon as Joe saw the bottle he fell flump off his chair on the floor.

NOVEMBER, 1957: Cut an ash s.e. of the house. It's covered with scale. This group seem never to have seeds, no young ones around. Another ash near the creek seeded heavily & had hundreds of seedlings. It was associated with Maples & Basswood. The unhealthy ones with Carolina Poplar.

MARCH, 1958: All this month light winds & fair. All signs of rain fail. Continues dry until Aug. Grass burnt up.

SEPTEMBER, 1958: A Dream: Long snowy road to s. horizon. Snake fences & distant elms. White winter sky. Road crowded with teams & men. I seemed to see it past the corner of Boyle's stretching s. up Morgans Hill.

MARCH 20, 1959: To J. Baker's for pump leathers. Real spring day. Hear Shore Larks & faint sound of falling snow crust. Hawks scream over the Maples. Ed reported this conversation between Carman C. (always gruff) & Mike Pickett (polite):
    Mike: 'Goodnight Carman.'
    Carman: 'Go to Hell.'
    Mike: 'You take them long trips yourself.'

OCTOBER, 1958: To Ox Narrows to saw wood. Fall colour through fog. Heavy showers all the time we're cutting. Trees shake down rain on us. Moosewood. Wild rock-ribbed country w. of Kinmount. No houses, no water, just thin bush on flat rock. The Canadian Shield.

JANUARY, 1959: A Dream: Just E. of Tisdale place, walking back from Concord. Passed through beautiful landscape, big roadside elms, wide green fields & slopes. A little old time house by the road, dark coloured. a black & white kitten on the grass. A square sign on the house bearing one word, WHEN. I looked in window & saw an old lady sewing & two younger ones reading. All this in very deep rich colours, green & browns, sunlit.

SEPTEMBER, 1959: With Willy K. to look at land by Minesing Swamp. Looked west at the view I liked so much nearly 50 years ago. Evening & hazy. W's land is nice open bush; bracken & asters under oak, pine, etc. Partridges, deer tracks. Very big white pine over 12′ circ. also Yellow Birch. Still in the bush after dark. Many worn out farms & spooky old houses in that area. W. pointed out a tall stone house in a low spot. An old lady lives there alone with 4′ of water permanently in cellar. She was walking around at the edge of the bush, tall & thin like her house.

NOVEMBER, 1959: To Minesing Swamp to measure Willy's land. Up & down hills all day long through woods & brush. All his land looks to the west across the swamp & towards the distant blue hills, what they call the Blue Mountains. Cloud shadows. We finished at sunset & went down in the swamp. Saw 2 deer run up the hillside through the oaks & red pine like 2 big dogs. In the low ground dead quiet. Big cedars, balsam & poplar very dense. Back on the railroad we heard voices & saw a dog. W. waited to catch hunters but they saw us & left the rifle in the thick woods. A fine looking boy told of many beavers down there. Later W. stopped a car with a man named Jim who carried an over & under gun. J. was a real swamp man, cheerful & pleasant but an awful drinker W. says.

MARCH, 1960: Ed & Frank have been up the back roads to see the big snow drifts. Ed says an old man named Murray lived back there. He had some very big steers. He was so fond of them he never would sell. He bought a Ford but never took it on the road. He blocked it up in the driving shed & used to race the engine & holler out 'Niagara Falls, Buffalo,' and so on. He fell dead between the house & the stable & his dogs stayed by him & let no one near.

OCTOBER 12, 1960: To Haliburton tax sale with A.M. First lot 10 miles on narrow but smooth bush road. Sandy & rocky woods with some good red & white pine. Sometimes a cabin in small grassy & rocky fields, some deserted & fallen in, others with a truck or a car alongside. Big hills of dark rock. Further south larger fields with stone piles, the whole rimmed with horizon of spruce &

poplar. Partridges fly up from dusting in the road. Most lots paid up before sale but 200 acres went for $60.00. House (old but large) & lot in village $125.00. A good home. Rocks look fire-blackened perhaps from cabin fires.

OCTOBER, 1960: To Albion Hills looking at land. Tongue-shaped hills, sandy & eroded. Went to an old brick house nicely set on a hillside overlooking a swamp & big wooded hill. Lady very stylishly dressed & made up but pleasant. Old gray nosed hounds curled up by the step. Found her husband back in the hills by a fine pond. The fall colours reflected richer & deeper in water.

MARCH 7, 1961: Yest. fine March day, high barometer but in afternoon sun ring & sun dogs. Today AM strong E. wind & low flying clouds. Wind reaches 70 mph, snow becomes med. blizzard, thunder rolls. By 11 PM quietens down but it's the eye only, bar. very low. Eye lasts till next eve. then strong N.W. wind & barometer starts to rise.

SEPTEMBER 13, 1961: Carla, Texas hurricane.

OCTOBER 31, 1961: A real November night, partly cloudy & still. Rays of Aurora but without movement. A heavy fall of white pine needles this year (& '62). What does it indicate, *if anything?*

NOVEMBER 1, 1961: Went with C. Schaefer to Thomson farm at Claremont. Fine view to East, sandy hills & woods. Grand sky of sun gleams on level clouds. Well-built stone house with one-sided front, only 1 window. Fierce dog but later made friends & coaxed us to throw apples for him to chase. Owner Edgar Evans appeared on tractor. His grandfather bought the farm from John Thomson & family there ever since. A very fine old brick house in Brougham.

NOVEMBER, 1961: Ed & Jim F. talked of a family that kept hired men on till paying up time then got rid of them. Dark stories. Jim said their boys liked to fight & picked on anyone who dared to walk along the Townline. One Sunday eve. Jim & Woods brothers went to Fisherville Church. After service they walked to the bridge

& the boys appeared, one with a gun. Started an argument. One of the Woods knocked them down & the other grabbed the gun & threw it in the creek.

Woods had a 'dandy little team of bays' and on a sleighing party one of the boys had some drinks & said he was going to drive. Woods knocked him backwards into the snow, speeded up the team & left him lying, hopefully to freeze.

DECEMBER 3, 1961: Sunday. Went to Willy's farm by Minesing Swamp. Around his little empty house the ground is trampled with deer tracks. We walked over his wheat which he thought looks poor but I thought fair. Willy says many times, 'I love this country.' I felt something strange & different there, character of the woods & individual trees, old & mysterious maybe from Indians. A deep portage trail runs through there from Nottawasaga R. to L. Simcoe.

JANUARY 3, 1962: Again at Willy's to look at 110 acres he wants to buy for $1500. About 15 acres cleared where the house was is covered with mulleins & other poor land weeds. Nice little poplar groves & in the woods some fine big birches, cedars, oaks. Many deer tracks, s.s. rabbits & fox tracks. Hear deer in the cedar swamp, then dead quiet. Porcupines have stripped some trees. Hydro surveyors have cut a line 6' wide & many fine trees lying left & right. We followed it a long way w. pulling up their stakes & heaving them far into the bush. He hates them he says. At dusk we left the swamp & went to Willy's neighbours as he was hungry. Cats came from under the stove & climbed on us. Mrs W. a slim dark girl has 5 boys. The oldest, 14, plays the accordian, another piano. She gave us supper then resumed ironing while the cats enjoyed the visitors. The two oldest boys ploughed & disked Willy's land for fall wheat.

JANUARY, 1962: Ed spoke of an old lady near Woodbridge, 'over 80 & she knows everybody's business from here to Hell & Owen Sound.'

JUNE, 1962: Ed & Jim Fisher helped Frank H. with his drilling rig

& with some work got him out of difficulty. He said nothing so as they left Ed called from the car, 'Thanks, Frank.'

JULY, 1962: Ed told about an old man named Brophy, worked for Tom Hughes at the hotel stable. When Brophy was harnessing the black horse it always picked his hat off his head & held it in his teeth. When Brophy finished he took his hat from the old horse & put it on again. Charged 10¢ to leave your horse there. One man refused to pay so B. scooped up the manure the horse left & shovelled it into the back of his buggy, 'If you leave no money, you'll leave naught else.'

AUGUST, 1962: Dry summer, grass killed, trees dying. Many things seem coming to an end. If anyone understands life probably they've not had much experience.

SEPTEMBER, 1962: In this late spell talked with Charlie Sinclair who runs the planing mill. He has seen snow in Thornhill every month but August. On Dominion Day 1903 they planned a big picnic but a few flakes of snow fell in the cold air.

OCTOBER, 1962: Fallen aspen leaves & light snow show up the tiny paths of cats & coons in the grass.

FEBRUARY, 1963: Ed told how John Pickett lost his dollar watch while shocking up grain. They hunted in vain & the field was fall ploughed. Next spring E. was seeding & found the watch behind the drill. It wouldn't start so he took the oil can from the drill & gave her a shot of oil. He shook it & away she went good as new. When he passed J's team he called, 'Want to buy a watch?' John carried it for long after.

Met Martha B. in the store. They were getting ready in the sugar bush she says. She still studies at home, modern history, etc. M. is one of those 'you wish to save from any waft of harm,' as the poet says.

APRIL, 1963: Lenticular clouds followed by cold & windy spell; snow melts on falling.

JULY, 1963: A Dream: Some ancient stone buildings in which some leaders were speaking of the loss of a battle. Then beautiful harp music & a woman's voice sings a lament. The voice soared up over the harp with a wonderfully sad effect.

SEPTEMBER 4, 1963: To Willy's Minesing farm to see corn & start mower engine. He has a 16 yr. old boy clearing brush in the fields overlooking the wonderful view west to the Blue Mountain. Smell of bracken, golden rod & asters. Old cellar hole & remains of a log barn, made of oak. People lived out their lives there, far from the road & neighbours but in sight of that view to the west & north. We walked a long way through the corn rows, feeling the heavy cobs. Much damage by coons. Willy says he shot 47. We drove through field trails & old logging roads to a tobacco farm. It looks prosperous, the owner sits in the house drinking all day. Black cat & red kitten playing & wrestling by the doorstep.

Returning to Willy's fields can't see his man on tractor though it's only 4:30. At the house where he stays we see the tractor parked & the boy inside watching T.V.

SEPTEMBER 12, 1963: Thunder then first snowflakes & frost. Aurora shines in my room like moonlight from N.W.

Amos B. told how they pulled down John Page's barn. Cut the tenons & took out braces then hitched on the big tractor. Just as Paul started to pull Isaac's dog ran into the barn. Amos yelled but Paul couldn't hear & down she came. The air pressure blew out a great cloud of dust on all sides. When things quieted down the dog crept out covered with dust. He crouched down till he knew which way was home then off hard as he could tear. Next morning they returned to find the chains stolen.

JANUARY, 1964: Cut the big elm stub by the highway. Very windy & cold. Willy has a new 18″ Stihl which performed wonderfully, sliced up the big log then ripped each round into 4 so we could get them on the truck. The stub was 50′ high x 40″ diam., about 120 rings.

MARCH, 1965: Jim often said, 'This world is not our home.' As you

64

get old you feel it more. People & environment changed, even weather not homelike.

OCTOBER, 1964: We had a visit from Gladys, widow of Max Von Hauser, & told again about her times on the bush farm at Nelly Lake. She was alone there while Max went to Austria. An English neighbour tried to scare her by knocking & refusing to identify himself. She shot the 30.30 through the door then opened it to find him trembling in the snow with his hands up. Another time an Indian came innocently enough & she then opened the door rifle in hand. He turned & ran, then when she put the gun back on the spikes it went off & she saw the poor Indian put on speed down the lake. The bullet ricocheted all around the log walls & went through all her clothes hanging in a row. Later she made friends with that Indian when he was making syrup in the maple bush. He had a little lean-to there & she was afraid the wolves might get him. But he said he didn't mind the wolves, she scared him the most.

One time A.Y. Jackson visited them & the Indian came to say that 'Hay Wire' Jackson was at the dock.

Her horse only came to the house at night & stood by the door sighing & snoring all night long. When morn came he ran into the bush to avoid work. She coaxed him into the barn with a pan of grain but he kicked the door down & away.

NOVEMBER 11, 1964: A wonderful fall, 6 weeks of fine autumn with little wind. You could live forever in such weather.

FEBRUARY 27, 1965: This week a heavy snowfall to 16". About 11 AM, no wind but snowing hard then came a rolling crash in the sky overhead. It rolled for a long time but no sign of lightning. Next day went to town with Willy. His old car overheats in the snow; it has no floor but W. has put in plywood. He has a couple of logging chains & some log tongs in the back for traction. 'We'll not get stuck!' Nor did we.

APRIL 4, 1965: Went with Willy to Credit Forks to see his elm cutting for M.DesB. A fine cool day, lots of snow. First we went to Barrie to pick up W's tractor which he lent to a neighbour. We found it in poor condition by their poor litle cabin. No woodpile. No pump. A boy fixing a truck by the house, a cigarette in one hand, beer bottle in the other. Alternating them to his mouth & now & then picking up a wrench. Doesn't know how Willy's tractor got in such a state, never did work right he says. Far beyond is the wonderful view across the swamp to Blue Hill. Looks as it did 50 years ago but then you know the devastation of the country by highways & hydro. W. loaded the tractor from a sand bank in the gravel pit & then went on to the Credit. On the river flats cheerful poplar groves. Some hundreds dead & infested elms cut & logs skidded, some of great size. W's men plan to make palettes from them for loading bricks & blocks. Silent there except for the smooth running river. Laurentian-like hills. Returning saw country that was snowcovered in morning now nearly bare. Small streams everywhere hurrying & reflecting the blue eastern sky.

SPRING, 1965: Reading J.M.'s notes I can see his lonely feeling & regret not sharing his interests more.

AUGUST 1, 1965: Julia's illness, first stroke. (Died Sept, 26, 1972, 6 AM) Mrs Albrecht, her Polish neice: 'It was a good book was read then, finished & closed.'

OCTOBER 27, 1967: A very symmetrical 12 hr. storm. Rain starts 10 AM. Eye passes over 1:30-2:30 & sun shines briefly then more rain & wind till about 10 PM. Rain stops & wind falls.

SEPTEMBER 24, 1970: Just before dark heard a continuous screaming of jays. Went out to see many hundreds. Trees & air filled with them all giving angry screams, as for an owl or hawk. Never saw such numbers nor heard such noise. New plants seen on our land.

Speedwell, Yellow Avens, Celandine, White Goldenrod, Broad leaves, Enchanters' Nightshade, Green Woodland Orchid, Bluets.

WINTER, 1976: Someone said I should try for an honourary degree. I already got an honour in Thornhill long ago before the days of chain saws. Jim Pearson had a bee to saw up a big tree close to his back door. I went on with one of the neighbours, all experienced sawyers. We know what to expect. After a while he began to tire & J. put on another. When I felt him slowing down I sped up so I got another partner. We finished the job & I heard one of them say, 'That Mac's a terror on the end of a saw.' & Jim answered, 'Yes sir, & you know what, he never eats meat, either.' The thing was I'd been sawing with a one man saw all winter while for the neighbours it was their first job of the season.

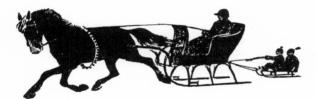

CHAPTER III

Two Stories: *Our Carpenter* and *Talks with a Hunter*

Our Carpenter: Our carpenter, Valerian Pavlovich, was a short, sturdy worker from southern Russia. His handsome face showed alert self reliance, ready for anything. He was very class conscious and spoke often of 'classical warfare' and 'concentrated camping.' But he had faith in no human government, for as he said, 'Honest man's very scarce. Communism never was come and never can come. People never grew up to it.'

He had taught himself to read English and at noon hour would spread a newspaper on his bench while he spelled out the world news. Then he would say, 'Come on, let's speak round the politician case. Situation very grave' (this he pronounced as gravy), and he would give his opinion with intelligence and insight. 'America all baseball, or else push peanut with him nose.' This he had really seen on the street in Buffalo and always cited it as typical American behaviour. Such things come from too much democracy he said.

Today he was firing up his little stove. 'I'm no good for this job because at home my old woman do it, she's never let me touch stove. Everything about the housekeeping case, that's for woman to do.' He needed a special moulding plane and took a worn out flat

file, stuck it in the fire to draw the temper then shaped and retempered it very expertly. While he worked he said, 'Watch well now and learn, or else you will be like that boy in the old country. His father's rich and sent him to learn how to be a blacksmith and after five years he says he knows it all. So he goes home and father gives him nice shop with tools, anvil, vice and all. Father says, "Well, son, what you make first?" Son says, "I'll make a hatchet." He puts the iron in the fire, blows, takes it out, bam, bam. It's too hot, the iron's burnt. He says, "You know father this iron's too small for the hatchet; I'll make a horseshoe." So again he heats it hot, hammers. Then he says, "Father I think I'll make a nail; this iron doesn't suit a horseshoe." Puts it in the fire, hammers, nail doesn't come. So he throw it in the water and it goes "Pfft." "See father," he says, "I make a 'Pfft'." "Yes, sonny" says father, "thats all you can make, you good for nothing."

'Some folks are all the time lazy, like the fly was sitting on the ox while its ploughing. Another fly comes along, says, "Hey neighbour, what you're doing?" First fly says, "Oh, today we're ploughing."

'Man, but I was a bad boy,' said Valerian Pavlovich pensively. rubbing his saw with a square of bacon rind. 'My little sister Sophie had a doll made of rags and I grabbed it and bit its head off. Oh, how she cried. Mama took the broom and give me a licking. She give me a licking once when I was twenty-two. I wanted to go to a dance. She said no. I said yes. She gave me good beating till I said, 'Enough Mama, I won't go.' She was very strong woman and looking very nice. When Sophie was born Mama was nine miles out in the bush getting berries. After baby was born she picked it up and her berries too and walked home, nine miles!'

Seeing some ladies with plenty of make-up: 'You know what I think of when I see them? An old rat in the mill house. He's just jump out of the flour and it's all over his face and whiskers, the old devil.' This word reminded him of Satan and eternal punishment. 'They said the devil will put you in a big tar lake. All my life I pass over the world and never see any kind of devil. Bad people yes, but no devil. When I was young fellow and crazy the priest told me the devil was maybe in the big swamp near our village. After I'd had a drink I'd go there with my dagger and yell, "Come on Devil and fight, you old son of a gun, come on and fight."But he never came.'

Another day, looking at a bearskin sent down from the north, Valerian said, 'What they want to shoot that bear for, he don't bother nobody. You see what a devil man is. He kills everything. One time I 'member I killed a squirrel. I took the gun and go for walk in the bush. The squirrel jumps, jumps, and runs up a tree, goes 'Tckk, Tckk.' I shoot and he's fall down and die. I think what the hell I killed him for. I threw down the gun and cried. Never killed anything else except wolves, the devils.

'One time in our village the women all go out to cut grain. They take their lunch and one old woman had a big jug of milk, maybe two gallon. Well, they put their lunch at the edge of the bush and work; wolf come out of the bush to grab some of the lunch and he stick his head right in the jug but can't get it out again. The women yell and throw stones. He run but can't see, bump against trees. They run up with sticks and rocks and kill him. He's very old, no teeth hardly.

'In that village,' said Valerian as he sharpened a plane iron, 'there's an old man, Leo. He knew what the weather would be for all year. He had it all cut on sticks, birch sticks. All the farmers go to him to see what weather will be and he was always right. He can't read but he can mark on the sticks and keep them all in a little shed by his house.'

Valerian was rip-sawing a piece of curly maple for violin backs. 'Look what Nature gives to us, that beautiful wood. Trees grow up, they look nice, smell nice. We should keep them like our eyes. But look at H. While the bush burns he makes politic speech, the damm fool.' Hepburn asked how he started cabinet work, 'I just learned myself, I always liked it. When I was little I made a violin and played it with a little branch for a bow with some hairs. I sit up on the stove and played. I made very nice little horses and sleigh, little harness too. Three neighbour boys, bad devils, they grab my horse and run home. I can't fight them all so I think what to do. I put some ashes in my pocket and went to their house. They're on the stove playing with my toy and they laugh at me. But all at once I take the ashes and throw it in their eyes, the biggest first and while they yelled I grab the horse and run home. It's cold, cold, middle of winter but I leave the door open and run through

the snow. Their mother came and told Mama and she says, "Well, I'll give him the strap but you must teach your boys not to steal his things.'"

I let the clock run down and told him it meant bad luck. He said, 'Don't believe that fanaticism, you'll be like old village woman in our country. Her son came home from America, new shoes, good suit, watch too. At night he left his watch in his vest on the table. Early morning, old woman's get up. She hears something, ch, ch, ch. She hears it in the vest, crosses herself, it must be a devil. Makes sign of cross more but ch, ch, never stops. She gets a big stick, throws the vest on the floor and hits it, bam, bam. The noise stops. She kneels down and thanks God she's destroyed that devil.'

Valerian Pavlovich then spoke of an afterlife. 'Nobody can't come back,' says he. 'I've walked over the world and never see nobody come back, never see no kind of ghost.'

I said that horses seemed to see ghosts sometimes. 'That's right. One time I'm riding by the cemetery at night, all quiet. All at once the horse stop, don't want to go ahead. I look, look, can't see nothing. I speak to the horse, try to make her go ahead, she's back up, shook all over. She's go to one side then jump ahead, but I can't see nothing.'

He said Cossacks when they try to catch new horses choose a cold, stormy day. They take those horses that face the storm and so get the strongest and bravest.

'Like I said, long time ago when I'm foolish and maybe had couple of drinks, I used to take my dagger and go in the dark swamp where I think maybe there's a devil and I'll yell, 'Come out, devil, and fight.' But you know what? One time in the army they let good men go away to work for one Lithuanian old man; make him some window frames. It's summer and awful hot in the house. I ask that old man can I sleep in the barn. He says, can't sleep in there because there's some kind of a devil there, they never go there at night. I'm laughing but the old man say everybody scared. Well, I don't say nothing to make him mad, don't want to argue, but I go to sleep there anyway. On one side of the barn there's clover, other side hay. I'm hook both doors so nobody can't get in and go sleep in the hay. Well, after a while I'm wake up, hear something in the clover go thump, thump. I yelled, 'Whatsa matter with you over there?' I'm lean up on my arm, can't see nothing. Then somebody throw big pile of clover on me. Then I'm get awful mad, because I think its neighbour boys called Kaslovsky. I jump up, grab my army belt and pull me out of hay onto the floor. I try to grab them and hit all around with belt. Can't find nothing. Go all 'round barn, can't see nobody. Well, all quiet then and I sleep till morning.

'The old man ask me, "Well, did you sleep OK?" I say, yes I

75

sleep. I never tell him nothing. I don't want to believe that fanata-cism.

'I slept there thirty-two nights and always the same program, thump, thump, and then pull me by the feet but I never see nothing. Old man see I'm tired because I don't sleep good and I tell him maybe Kaslovsky boys try to scare me. But he says if you gave them boys big piles of money they won't go in that barn at night. They know there's some kind of devil there. You know what? I think maybe I must have been lunatical from the moon. Anyway, that's true story, but I never see nothing.'

Said Valerian Pavlovich as he dipped a chisel in a can of water and moved it gently over the whetstone. 'You know what? If only I had another horse like the one we had in Old Country I'd be a big man. All red with dark stripe down her back. She had two sons, but wolves, the devils, they killed one. My father was no good, a drunkard, but he very liked that horse. One time she went nearly seventy miles in four hours.' This I couldn't believe but the old man insisted. 'Sure, that's right. I remember that time good, because there's a crust on the snow & when she turned out to pass other sleighs it cut her legs. But my father, old devil, he's drunk and never notice. Next day he see her cut legs and cried but too late then.

'After that she's get thin and go thinner, thinner every day. My father sold her to a Jew, but a good one. He's feed her up, soon she's well and fat again. But my father can't live without that horse. He's say to the Jew, "Sell me back my horse." He have to pay three times what the Jew give him but he had the horse again.

'She's not very big but long, and, Holy Moses, she can pull. One time in the Spring, roads are terrible but my father's take some rye to town, 30 proods. One place, exactly in the bush, there's a big hole of mud and there's a nobleman's carriage stuck there with three horses. There's men pushing but can't get out. Well, our horse, she's keep on pulling hard and go 'round the carriage but my father's stop her for little rest. Then this nobleman (sort of a big-shot, you know) he yells out, "Ho, farmer, how much you get on your wagon?" "O 'bout 30 proods." "You must have strong horse to take that on these roads." My father yells, "Sure, and she can pull your carriage out too." Big-shot he's laugh and say, "How, when my three horses can't move it? But I'll give you three rubles to pull me out."

'So father's unhitch our horse and put her on nobleman's carriage and she can't wait, she's all the time dancing in one place. Then my father's let her go and she's blow through her nose & jump, mud fly all 'round but she's take the carriage out and take it right up the hill. The big-shot want to buy her but father say, "No, never I'll sell that horse."

'I 'member one time I'd been to town with some linning and I had money to take home. 'Round that place there's lots of robbers, they stop you on the road, take your money. Well, I ride along in the bush and there's a deep valley and stream with bridge and then the road goes up between high banks.

'Now it's nearly dark and when I go to the bridge I see something moving by the bank of the road. Then I see exactly where these banks are a spruce tree put across the road. Then I know its some robbers so I make the horse go and she's run like the devil up the hill and jump right through the spruce tree. Robbers shoot but don't hit nothing. They jump out and one grab my leg but I hit him with my whipper exactly in the eyes and he's drop off.

'Horse keep running like the devil home but when I get off at the barn I see a big splinter right stuck in her chest, a broken branch from that spruce. I have to take the pliers and jerk it out then I wash it with iodine. But anyway can't the horse work for three days.

'I remember,' said Valerian Pavlovich between strokes of his mallet as he pounded away cutting dovetails, 'When I was a little boy staying at my Grandfather's, they had there at the nobleman's house a bear, and she's very smart. He can carry wood & water to the house.' I looked doubtful at this. 'Yes, that's right,' insisted the old man, 'He carried wood to the back porch and two pails of water on a yoke. He's do that every day.

'The men used to wrestle with him and he wouldn't hurt them long as they put him down just once, but if they try to do it the second time, Good-bye boy! One evening my Grandfather's sitting on the steps of his shop (He's cabinet maker like me) and the blacksmith with him. Exactly then is coming that bear carrying water on the yoke and he have to pass right in front of them. The blacksmith's pick up some shavings and throw them in the water. Grandfather's says, 'No, don't; be careful,' but the blacksmith laugh, he's often wrestle with the bear, he's not scared. But the bear jump & hit him on the back and hurt him inside. He can't work for a long time.

'Did he do anything to the bear? No, why? It's not him's fault. But one time the hunting dogs chase him and he's jump on the woodpile and start to throw chunks of wood at the dogs. The Lady's little dog is there and a piece hit him and killed him. She made them shoot the poor bear.'

Talks with a Hunter: 1. ON FOXES Well sir (said my hunter friend as he gloomily counted over his few remaining shells), I see where the township has paid out bounties on more'n fifty foxes. Now to my mind that's money wasted. There's always plenty of fellows like myself, only too willing to loaf 'round the fence corners looking for foxes without getting paid for it. Sure, I know they say the foxes get the pheasants and steal chickens. I never keep the blamed things myself so I wouldn't know but whenever you hear of some-body losing a bunch of hens it's always 'way over in Whitchurch or some blank place miles away. If they had a dog with any sense he'd keep the fox off. As for pheasants they're a new thing but I've walked the fields and woods for forty years and I only seen one place where they'd caught a pheasant. Most likely it was starving to death. Anyhow, they're welcome to a few for all I care. Just as soon they'd have 'em as some of those guys that come out from town. Boy, are they something.

Why, I was reading the other night where a fellow says most of the harm they blame on foxes is done by loose dogs. Over in Illinois where he lives foxes are protected and he says all the game is extra thick there (see *Outdoor Life*, February, 1941). You know blamed well if a fox could talk and you asked him what his diet was he'd holler 'Mice' and it would be the truth too. You know yourself how mice breed. Why, I heard one of those scientific lads on the radio one time and he said one pair of mice could breed thousands in next to no time and eat tons of grain and hay. I tell you boy, when you've paid good money for apple trees and raised them to bearing, then find them ringed by mice, that's when you'll wish the old fox had been around. That's when you wonder about all that bounty money. Yes sir.

One poor sap told me how he'd found chickens 'round the fox's den so they must be bad. Blamed if they weren't some that had died 'way back in the fall and got spread out with the manure. A fox'll pick up anything like that.

Well sir, to my mind, a few foxes are a good thing and I'll be sorry to see them all shot off. Just the same, I like to take after them now and again, but that's no reason every whipper-snapper should be out blasting away. Leave it to us old guys with some sense.

2. ON SQUIRRELS: I'll tell you one critter I haven't much use for (said the old hunter, taking down an antique lever action .22) and that's them red squirrels. Yes sir, I can get along without them, and I figure on thinning out the squirrel population right now. I always say there's mighty few animals that don't do some good and squirrels are all right in a big piece of bush. You know yourself how they bury nuts and acorns and help plant up the forest. But just 'round the house in shade trees they're no more use than a skunk in Sunday School.

You can see how the birds hate them. One time I saw a jay after a squirrel and he jumped from the old snow apple into that spruce. Just when he hit the spruce the jay grabbed his tail and jerked him right off the limb so he hit the ground kerblam. You don't often see one fall. But once I seen one with a young bird and I chased him along 'till he run up the roof and out on that gable. Well sir, he didn't know where else to go so he dropped the bird and jumped clear off the peak of the roof down on the road. Heck no, he wasn't hurt, he jist parachuted down with his tail. That's one thing certain, a squirrel can't live without his tail. I bet he'd die in a month especially in cold weather. It's his parachute, his rudder, and his blanket too.

I mind once long before your time, an old dog we had, kind of

80

a yellow collie. We were up by that little swamp where all them turtles used to be. Well, there's kind of an old stub leaning out over that green water and this dog he chased a squirrel up this stub. They went hell-a-hootn' right to the top and the squirrel just sailed off like one of these here gliders and lit on the other bank. But the old dog he stuck there and couldn't get down, it was too steep. At last he flopped off into the water and came out all over green scum.

Another year there was a couple of the little devils over by that west line and blamed if they didn't start gnawing the bark off those maples there. They got a lot of limbs stripped white in no time but I soon put the kibosh on them. You got to draw the line somewhere. Trouble is, there's not enough hawks and owls to keep 'em down. Up north they say the martins do away with a lot, follow 'em through trees 'till they come up with them. Pity there's no martins around here, that's what I say.

---

3. ON MUSKRATS: Now you take muskrats (said the old hunter, squinting down the land towards the swamp), it beats all how they've been thinned out just around here. You mind last year there was four rat houses down in the swamp and there's none this year. It's those blank dogs cleaned them out and nobody got the good of them either.

Why, I mind one spring morning years ago, I walked up the creek just from the dam to that cedar that grows out of the stump, not more'n fifty rod and I counted 24 muskrats. Now you'll never see one hardly. Because there's no cover for them. They don't need much water but they want cover. One time I seen a muskrat travelling across the flats down there and I took after him. He dived into a little bit of a puddle about 8 inches deep, and man, he kicked up the mud and leaves so I never saw him again.

Yes siree, I knew a young chap had a drainage ditch through his farm just about 2 feet wide and he got enough rats out of there to help pay for a course at Guelph. No, I never went in much for trapping them. I'm not hard up and they never done me any harm. But you get them cornered up, and they're fighters. Yes sir, they'll fight to the last. One day in the winter I came on one in that little field back of the barn and I tell you boy, he faced me ready to go for me. I had a fork but heck, I didn't bother him. I never did believe in killing everything you see and I like to see them show some spunk. You take when a mink corners them they'll never give in. Yes and maybe an extra tough muskrat will get the best of it after all. Now and again a heron will spear one, young ones most likely.

They say the Indians spear them through clear ice. I never saw that myself but one winter up north some rats had a house on a stump in a deep pond and I'd go up and give it a tap and see them shoot out under the ice.

You mind those down in the swamp last year. They started building away back in summer and they worked like heck until by fall they had their houses three feet high and all set for cold weather. No sir, they don't put off their work like some I could name, they keep right after it. Yep, as I look at it they're hardworking, spunky little critters and they don't bother me. far as shooting them goes, there's no sport in that, no more'n shooting at a fur hat.

4. ON COONS: Well sir (said the old hunter as he looked along a hollow basswood cut and left by the loggers), well sir, I mind the day when five coons lived in that tree. It's a caution how scarce they are nowadays. They've been hunted out and another thing is there's mighty few den trees left for them. Every sport likes a coon hunt but blamed few would ever take the trouble to put up a den and maybe get some coons to settle down. I tell you boy, coon hunts will be a thing of the past when you're my age. Now I was reading on Sunday about a fellow who put up fifty boxes for coons and 'twasn't long before he had coons in some of them. And they weren't all in heavy bush either, just along the fences in odd trees. Now there's a man deserves to go coon hunting. But these fellows that shoot and shoot and never do a blank thing to keep up the stock of game, I got no use for them.

Well, as I was saying, you got to hand it to a coon. He don't look for fights but he'll take on three or four dogs, every one twice as big as he is, and if there weren't a couple of men to back up the dogs he'd likely send them kiting. Yes sir, if coons had fair play there'd be mighty few ever killed by dogs. Why, when I was a little gaffer there was lots of coons. You'd hear them most any fall night singing away like a bunch of owls. I've come on them right in daylight and they'd just walk along, peaceful as preachers, then up a big maple and all the time eyeing me over their shoulder. They knew I was too small to bother them. One time I was in the swamp after the cows and I saw one washing a crawfish (you know how they wash everything they eat, even a frog). Well he sloshed this up and down in the creek and all the time he kept looking around at the trees and sky as calm as could be.

That's all a thing of the past. Nowadays if a coon shows up there's lots ready to shoot it down, in season or out, and maybe it's got young ones somewhere to starve to death. Of course a coon will eat anything and maybe they get an odd hen now and again for they're great hands at getting in anyplace. Just the same they do plenty more good than harm, eating mice and all sorts of bugs and grubs. I tell you I'll be sorry to see them killed out and if we don't watch our step that's just what's going to happen.

5. ON HUNTERS: There goes a couple more lads with guns, said the old hunter looking out the woodshed door. Well sir, war or no war, I never saw so many hunters as nowadays. Of course you can't call every man with a gun a hunter. These guys that go around busting fences and pulling off rails and shooting everything that moves, they're no hunters, only killers. Now you take a real hunter, he's got to have brains. A fellow can't associate with animals long without getting some sense. He looks after the other fellow's property and shuts the gates and he don't scare the stock or cause any trouble. Another thing, he takes care of the game too, dosn't shoot out of season and on his own place he keeps up a bit of cover. He knows blame well that if he doesn't, game's going to be scarce and you know it's scarce enough already. another few years and it'll be gone unless we're mighty careful.

It's no use blaming the foxes or hawks or owls. To my mind you can't have healthy game without a fox or so to pick up any sick ones, and that's not just my own idea neither. Lots of men with more brains than me think the same. Like down south there in the States, somebody got the notion the hawks were taking the quail. So they started cleaning out the hawks, but blame it all, there was less quail than ever. The cotton rats got the eggs and young birds and it was the hawks that had kept the rats down. Yes sir, the whole works sort of dovetails in together and when you start monkeying with one part it's all liable to fall apart.

As long as there's cover and what they need to eat there'll be game, that is if we don't wear it out with hunting. Give it a chance to rest up and eat now and again. And let me tell you boy, when you go on another man's land, watch your step and handle everything extra careful, else you're no hunter, just a nuisance and the best game for you to shoot would be yourself.

CHAPTER IV

Letters to Doris Heustis Mills

August 2, 1923

Mrs Mills said I might write if I thought of anything. I like to write anyway. Perhaps I can make a sort of report. The family are all well. Father talks of Michaelangelo & Madonnas & prophets etc. most of the time. He has been reading some letters of Emerson & Carlyle to us. Mother is reading Memories of Hawthorne so we should know something about the Concord group soon. But our dear old Henry was the most interesting of all. I have just read a book on him by Mark van Doren but didn't like it. They argue about his ideals & objects in life but I think his one object was to live the best life he could in every way. Did you know that when he died he left three thousand pages of notes for a book on Indians? He was a great worker. Somewhere he says,

> My life was the poem I would have writ
> But I could not both live & utter it.

Today, Friday, is fine & clear after rain. Should be nice at the Ocean. We can see the blue hills away up the valley.

> Their far blue eye
> A remnant of the sky.

Last Sunday Miss Dawson & Mr Chates visited us. Mr Sekido

DORIS HEUSTIS MILLS began painting in 1922 and shared atelier space with Thoreau in the Toronto Studio Building. In 1926, 1928, 1930 and 1931 she was invited to exhibit with the Group of Seven at the Toronto Art Gallery. Married to Dr J. Murray Speirs in 1941, she has since become well-known as an ornithologist and recently edited the autobiography of Margaret Morse Nice, *Research Is a Passion With Me*.

has been having his troubles but is getting on alright now. He is sitting on the floor now gazing up at his picture. I am at the Studio, this letter has been spread over some time.

I see some nice pines coming down. They look the most innocent of all the trees. Harvest is on now & is getting rid of some of the green in the landscape. I have made only 3 tries at sketching since you left. I hope the ocean does not seem too large.

I received a nice note from Mrs Mills Sr. As Henry says, 'Yours for remembering all good things.'

July 11, 1928

. . . I wonder where you are now. Here the sun shines, the wind blows & the poplars sparkle.

. . . I wonder how the turtles enjoy touring. If the children keep them in a basin or something they will need some stones to rest on. I think the sun will make their shells harder. Ultra-violet, you know. They have lately discovered new light, called the Cosmic Rays. It will go through 20 feet of steel as easily as through glass. They are not visible to our eyes.

All went well today; I had the so-called conference & got nicely smoked up. You might think I was a real business man.

I would like to find some arrow heads at Concord. H. found so many. See if you see any next time. I wonder if you have felt like painting. Never mind if you don't for people who live beautifully don't need to. But it would be nice to see some if you felt like it.

I must take some money out to the old folks. Here is a miserable little drawing. I will try & send some better.

July 13, 1928

This has been a busy day & as I must do a little more tonight I thought I'd take a rest by writing to you a little. Today I was at another smoking bee & met Mr Geo. H. Doran of New York, a very nice old man. No one offered me a smoke but I didn't get offended.

Now you will be really at the sea. 'Roll on thou deep & dark blue Ocean, roll.' Today it is raining here, very getly & softly & the robins sing. I think & wonder what . . . kind of country & trees & birds you are seeing. Last night I went to Thornhill & found all well & this AM my father got back from NYC much 'spenified.' He had a wonderful time & went through dozens of buildings, up the Sherry-Netherland tower & inspected the $40,000 a year apartments, etc. He saw Sekido too. He brought me a little Egyptian hawk from the Metropolitan (see tracing), a very unusual thing for him. It is plaster. He enjoyed it a lot & likes the New Yorkers, stayed at the Roosevelt Hotel & really seemed quite renewed.

I have just read 'The Steppe' by A. Chekov, a wonderful story; wish I had another. Yesterday I was at the Reference Library & saw a book on Psychology of Behaviour & looked at a chapter dealing with things I often worry about. I thought, my, this man has some good ideas, just what I think myself. I felt quite cheered & enlightened. When I looked to see who the man was I saw the author's name – Elizabeth Severn, so then I knew why I liked it.

I seem to talk a lot about myself but I haven't seen many people I know . . . I will send some drawings soon. Mr Doran asked me to let him see some tomorrow. Wonder what kind of thing he likes.

Yesterday was H.D.T.'s birthday.

July 18, 1928

This has been a very, what you call, *hectic* day. Five drawings from Sampson-Matthews to go to Montreal tonight. But they're finished now.

My father is working hard on his building. It will be a very interesting one. It will have gold & colour decoration at the top & inside, mosaics. In the hall they are having quotations from Canadian poets for the people to read while they wait for elevators. It is 18 stories high, not much for NYC.

I wish I could go down to the sea too, if only I had a car, but as the poet says — 'such dreams are vain.' I just paid $200 on the old folks' mortgage so that's settled & I'm glad.

On Sunday I tried to take a picture of the clouds; they were so wonderful but of course they didn't turn out well. See enclosed. I covered up that wretched shed with the car, so here you see our old New England homestead. No sign of Marion's picture.

I guess I must go now & take the last of the drawings to Mr Sampson. I thought they looked rather nice. They are Quebec, Alaska, Canadian Rockies, & By the Sea.

July 19, 1928

I just got your note about the painting etc. Just think, 2 pictures in one day. That's wonderful. About the colour, I feel quite sure it's all right. Better than ever. I think that quiet, what you call chalky colour is really a sign of advancing in every way. The gentlest are the strongest. The best pictures are ever the quietest & they live longest & help us most. Everything as it advances seems to become more serene, peaceful & gentle. Don't you feel that even Lawren's colours are quieter lately? The Lord reigneth, even in painting. Perhaps this doesn't sound very practical & helpful but you know I mean it. If the pictures give you the feeling you had it doesn't matter a bit about the colour. I'm no expert you know so I can't tell you what colours to use but I know your work always gets better & better, clearer & clearer. The design is the great thing not the colour. I wonder if you have a frame. I expect your white walls don't help the pictures very much. I look forward to seeing them.

July 22, 1928

. . . This is me at a meeting with leading publishers & looking wise. They are trying to get me to go to New York but nothing doing. Mr Doran is directing the ads now so that's better. I have made one of MacKenzie at the Pacific . . . but I won't talk about that anymore.

I took my camera to Thornhill & used a roll of film & will send any that look good enough. I'm also sending a few proofs & draw-

ings with regrets that they're not better. . . . Mr Doran thought T.M.'s work very distinguished but rather cold. Frigidaire.

July 25, 1928

. . . I'm still struggling with the Makers of Canada & have drawn Madelaine de Vercheres & Champlain on Georgian Bay. I'll be glad to see the last of all our National Heroes. How is the painting now I wonder? Is the Conception still beyond the Execution? Well then, all's well.

 . . . You spoke of reading Chekov but I think you might not like those stories. Lots I don't like but some are wonderful. I guess Chekov isn't your kind of writer. Last night I read some of Dorothy Wordsworth's Journal. She was a dear & one of the best that ever was. Much better than her brother, but then sisters are always best I think.

 . . . We have so many Hollyhocks at the Studio this year, when you look out it's like a Garden party with pink & white dresses.

July 26, 1928

. . . I met Mrs Mills Senior on the car today & she talked very kindly to me all the way down town. The Houssers leave on August 1 but I haven't seen them yet, I guess they're busy. I just read Judge Lindsey's book, 'The Revolt of Modern Youth'; I'm not sure what you would think of it. I thought it was good & it expresses many things I thought out for myself long ago. He is a good man.

. . . L.W. asked me to look at his new sculpture, a head of Christ. I didn't know what to say & only thought 'Goodnight! Ain't Art Horrible?' But it seems nice to L. & he enjoys his work so all serene.

. . . I've dropped the History for a little while & am working for Louis Carrier. Last night there was a fine storm & I lay watching it for a long time. Grand crashes & flashes to light up the tossing trees & rain. Beautiful.

July 29, 1928

A wonderful cool, bright day with your favourite clouds. . . . Yesterday I went to the Island again & I saw a yacht race, a seaplane, flocks of kingfishers, & people of every type. Returning it was very windy, with big gray waves & I saw the Life Savers go out & save some people whose boat upset. It was very thrilling to see their big speed boat flying along & shooting up fountains of spray. So you can see I was out seeing all the sights of the Venice of Toronto. Going over I sat with all the sporty yachtsmen & heard one tell about his sailing stunts. But how sad, for by the time we got across he was seasick. There must be a moral in that somewhere.

The Houssers leave this week & they have asked me up this eve, which was kind of them. I have been getting Sekido's book typed & have been interested to see how the stenographers enjoyed

93

it. They are a real type of typist. The head one very efficient, horn-rimmed glasses & everything. Her assistant, a flapper named Pat who says 'all rightie.' They say they are very busy, so many people are writing books & stories & wanting them typed.

How are you getting along with Political Economy? I guess Mr Shaw would be too deep for me. I have got a bad habit of reading fast & carelessly. I'm still on the Chekov craze & have now finished 7 of the 10 volumes. Some of them make me tired & others seem like stories Jesus might have written if he had gone in for fiction. Such insight & sympathy. It is the first time I have laughed for ever so long. and some are very painful, like 'The Party.' I think I told you about Judge Lindsey's 'Revolt of Modern Youth'; I admired it & liked it for I've always liked him. When I tour the States I think I'll call on him in Denver. . . .

August 3, 1928

Ever since 6 o'clock it has been thundering & raining & still is with Blue lightning. Some people near have just been singing, I thought quite beautifully. A lady with a very pure voice, & two men. While the lightning opened & shut its wings in the north. I wish I could play & sing too. But T.M. is a dumbbell. He never draws or paints or writes, only sleeps & eats. When I was watching the men laying the marble in the new bank today I saw that one had a bouquet of flowers in a milk bottle. It looked wonderful & affecting there in all the confusion, & a sort of presence.

. . . The other day I felt discouraged for a minute when I heard a little girl near here say — 'I'm scared of him,' — & I realized I have a sort of mean expression. But it's only because I feel rather sad & I always liked that little girl.

> My face I don't mind it,
> For I am behind it.
> It's the people in front that I jar.

So now I try not to look gloomy when I see any children coming. I didn't get Mr Shaw's book after all as I didn't like to ask. Turgenev is my favourite author & I'm sending him again. 'O native land of long-suffering/Land of the Russian people.' Thanks for the stamp information. I just thought I'd be on the safe side. Now I'll be able to buy an ice cream cone.

August 5, 1928

. . . I have't been out yet today having been busy on Sir Joseph's birthday present. I expect he would not approve of Sunday work. But I am an utter heathen, God forgive me. I have faithfully started a very little picture, 12 x 9″. It looks very discouraging right now. It is Mary & Jesus out walking. It needs your eye of faith to look at it I guess.

. . . I have been reading the bird book you lent me, also Sir E. Gray's 'Charm of Birds' & White's 'Nautral History of Selbourne.' There are too many new books to read. Miss Ruth Suckow's 'The Bonney Family,' & 'The Son' by Hildur Dixelius which is the second part of the 'Minister's Daughter.' Sara Alelia was a Saint, I think. There are so many, aren't there?

I hope you get out to Concord. H.D.T. would be disappointed otherwise. I give him large mental hugs every day.

August 6, 1928

Such weather we're having. Pouring rains, gray clouds & sea mists. It's almost like being on a holiday. Yesterday I went to Thornhill & saw all the people, played croquet in the drizzle & so on. One of the girls I went to school with there is being married today & I've had her on my mind. Hope she will be happy for she was gentle & good.

    . . . Today was Civic Holiday & in the afternoon I went out to High Park for a little while. Too many people to stay long. Ball games, ukeleles, picnics, etc. I saw some beautiful little Blue-bells. Down by the pond were rows of fishermen, knee deep in the weeds & poison ivy & throwing their little floats out into the water. Then they wait a while & draw up a load of weeds & mud. No one caught any fish. I guess they were not casting on the right side. I pretended I was H.D.T. at Walden & sat under an oak & read. I am reading Tess again with my usual groans & sighs. Poor, dear Tessie. She was an angel. I wished I could have had a canoe on the pond. But I can't swim. My education was very poor. & too tired to learn now. Sekido is having a nice time in Los Angeles & says already he feels very strong from fresh air. He sails for Japan September 6. I hope he praises up his wife as she deserves when he gets home.

CHAPTER V

Letters to Carl Schaefer

Studio Building, Severn Street,
December 17, 1924

Is this how I should address you? I was really pleased to get you
letter. Many thanks. Glad to hear about the pen and ink drawings.
I guess there is nothing like drawing for a foundation of painting. I
would like to see some of yours.

I had a note from Sekido too but without much news. I didn't
see the Exhibition you speak of but I saw the O.S.A. small pictures

CARL SCHAEFER became a close friend of Thoreau's when he studied
under and worked for Thoreau's father, J.E.H. MacDonald. Well-known
as a water colourist and oil painter he became a member of Canadian
Society of Painters in Water Colour in 1933 and a charter member of
Canadian Group of Painters in 1936. In 1940 he became the first Canadian
to be awarded a Guggenheim Fellowship and in 1978 he was appointed
Member of the Order of Canada.

& a view of Posters at the Gallery. Some of these were fine. Lots of *design* in them. Hope you will come down for the Group of 7 show. It opens January 9. The Group is getting out a portfolio of drawings at the same time. 20 signed prints in each one & they should be fine I think.

Please come & see us if you get down any time & perhaps bring some more sketches. My Father is trying to paint these days. As yet he has only one large one finished. 'Rain in the Mountains.' All kind of flat & simple. About 5 x 6'. I'm glad about design in your work. Design is thought & that's the main thing in pictures & everything I guess.

Perhaps you haven't seen this catalogue.

Studio Building,
Severn Street, January 19, 1925

I was glad to get the woodcut & I like it fine. About the sky, I think it might have been a little darker above the roofs & lighter in the top right corner. Something like enclosed sketch. So as to bring out the white roofs more against the sky. But it is too late to do this now so perhaps the dark part of the sky might have a few cuts in it to make it more of a gray, though I like it as it is all right. The lower parts are great & only fault I see is that the roofs don't contrast quite enough with the light sky. Sometimes you can fix up a print with a brush like this. Sorry to spoil your print but it will show what I mean. Here are a few cuts I thought were on the same lines though of course they were done on wood I suppose. I have made only one little one this winter. Meant for rocks by a frozen lake. The Group show is only on during January as the Graphics Arts is having an Ex. in February It really is fine. I liked especially some of Mr Harris' mountains. More abstract I think & very carefully thought out. They have one room of Black & Whites, & the Portfolio looks good too. I send a *Can. Forum* with an article by A.Y. Jackson also drawing by J.E.H.M. & cover by T.M.

Hope you keep on with the woodcuts. Thanks for sending it.

This is the label I made for the Portfolio.

Studio Building, Severn Street,
April 7, 1925

Yours rec'd with many thanks. I like the letterhead. I haven't much
news to tell. The other day I saw the exhibition of British pictures
at the Gallery. It seemed bright and very interesting but nothing
impressive I thought. Lots of painting ability. Perhaps not enough
Nature. I think the Nash brothers had most. The most modern
things were usually the most carefully done, some very detailed. I
like them that way with no problems avoided or sketched over. A
lot of big names are there, often the least interesting. I wouldn't
bother looking at Frank Brangwyn. There are also small shows at
Eatons & Simpsons.

The Art School is working hard on the Masquerade. I don't
attend not being a student & no good for social events anyway.

There is a Russian Show coming to the Gallery next which
should be fine. I like them & Scandinavian.

Glad you are painting some. I would like to try as well. Here
are a couple of cuts from papers that looked interesting.

Studio Building,
Severn Street, Toronto,
June 10, 1925

I should have written long ago but hoped to have something
interesting to say. About your drawing . . . I don't know what
makes them so slow but my father also hasn't been paid for a little
picture he sold. I suppose it will be straightened out sometime.

There has been a Russian show which was very interesting. It
had quite a Canadian character. There is one family portrait,
Father, Mother, & little boy very fine, which they have been trying
to buy for Toronto. Must be fine to be able to do portraits. Ever try
any? I don't mean Mr Grier's kind so much. Are you getting out
now? I expect to go to Lake Simcoe for a little while. You can see
the sky there anyway. How are your ideas on Art? Let's have

design & imagination. I like pictures that make me want to improve my ways. Ones that have lots of thought in them.

Here is a little account my father wrote of his last trip.

Do you ever think of writing anything? Perhaps something like your letter about the Germans.

Studio Building, Severn Street,
Toronto, July 16, 1925

Yours rec'd with thanks. I'm glad to hear you are writing. Better than painting I think. I was at Lake Simcoe only a few days & did nothing in the Art line. Since then we were at Coboconk for a week, wild country, rocky & interesting but not big. But I like any country almost if only it is wild & not crowded. My father made a dozen sketches there. He thinks of going again to the Rockies. About writing, do you ever read anything of Henry D. Thoreau's? Great, I think. He wrote *Walden,* or *Life in the Woods, A Week on the Concord, The Maine Woods,* etc. Also kept a Journal or Diary, a good idea I think. He & Mr Emerson are my great admirations. I enclose a few extracts from his books. Mr Jackson made the bookplate.

I would like to see some writing sometime if you didn't mind showing it.

Sorry this isn't the one of H.D.T.'s I meant to send but I find I haven't it.

Sunday,
August 16, 1925

Yours rec'd. That must be interesting work in the country. You won't mind if I send this old book? I had two. Perhaps it will interest you in parts. There are fine ideas in it, though they are only extracts.

My father is soon leaving for the West. Mr Harris & Mr F.

Carmichael go to Coldwell on Lake Superior. I did send 3 pen drawings to the c.n.e. They were rather queer. Titles were 'Wild Geese by the shore,' 'Island & moonlight,' & 'Loons under water.' I will look for something of yours. Wonder if you got paid for that little drawing. I see it at their house, hanging by a Rockwell Kent.

Studio Building,
August 29, 1925

I enjoyed your writing. Thanks for letting me see it.
    Here is a c.n.e. Catalogue.
    They say the Russians are grand.

Studio Building, Severn Street,
July 8, 1927

Your letter rec'd this morning. We are still in Town sure enough & will be I guess for a while.

How are you? All right I hope. Sorry you feel lonely. Mr Jackson leaves today for a trip to the Arctic with a Government expedition. He should make interesting things up there, Ellesmere Island, Baffin Land etc. Mr Harris is taking his family to Temagami. I'm glad you're making drawings. Have you any that would do for *The Forum*? I like the house you enclose. Perhaps you would send down a few.

I have done very little in the Art line except a few drawings of birds, etc. We have been designing bronze letters for Manufacturer's Life Building.

I think Mr Lismer is pretty sure to remain in Toronto. He expects to paint more.

Lowrie tells me you are married. That's nice.

I hope you have some drawing we could use. It's hard to get them as the artist doesn't get anything but honour.

I'm sorry not to write a better letter.

Toronto, August 3, 1927

I'll keep the drawings a few days longer if you don't mind. I would like to put one in *The Forum* but I don't know for sure. *The Forum* editors are not very fond of really modern Art. I like the ones 'Hills' & 'Bright Sun' best.

I don't know much about the show in Paris. I think they are going to translate & print the French press comments if it isn't already done. If I see them I'll let you know. I think everything went well.

I guess I'll send a couple of drawings to the c.n.e. too. Mr Haines is going to have a group of Canadian black & whites.

I call these people Mr having known some of them when I was little & got the habit then. Did I tell you they have some good Canadian pictures at the Grange? It is a summer show, not new things but good ones like 'Above Lake Superior.' Also a lot of Tom Thomson sketches. I don't know very much Art news I'm afraid. L.W. is often working hard down in the basement, modelling. I'm always working on commercial things. I think *The Forum* is having an article on the Paris show by Eric Brown. Just remembered this.

Are your drawings framed? I could lend you frames if you wish. Have you seen a Studio special number, 'The Woodcut of Today'? It's worth buying I think.

25 Severn Street,
Toronto, November 1, 1927

Thanks for your letter & photos. I didn't like Mr B's drawing much either. However it made variety.

Dr Banting's sketches were not very exciting though some were good in their own way. Mr Lismer's sketches of Lake Superior are fine, different from any one else who has been there. I only saw them a few minutes. My father is trying to paint these days but has little time. I see the advance Xmas Cards are out & still look for yours. This is great weather for being out of Toronto. Almost wish I was a duck hunter.

February 29, 1928

Sorry to be so long in thanking you for your woodcut. I've been hoping to go to the Group show so I could say something about it. I'm ashamed to say I wasn't down at all except once before it was ready. However here's a catalogue if you haven't seen one. The show got some grand knocks in the papers I think, perhaps you read them. Mr George Russell, 'A.E.,' the celebrated Irish writer was here & said he thought it was the most interesting & significant thing he had seen in America. That's more than I think. He is a painter too, also an economist, a good combination. But I expect you know about him.

I've been busy doing a lot of lettering, not interesting but it takes a lot of time. I hadn't anything to try on the o.s.a. but Lowrie sent several & some sculpture. I see the little cards arriving today, '25 of your works have been accepted' etc. There was a picture of the Committee in this morning's Globe.

Thornhill,
December 31, 1935

Just a word of thanks for the basket. It was much appreciated by all. We passed the holiday season in sawing, splitting & hauling wood from our poor old elm. I had to buy myself a one man crosscut saw. (4.95)

Bringing home Ye Olde Yule Loge.

I guess the good old Mutual Benefit Group is about ready for their Show which opens Friday. I have heard nothing further about sending anything. Have nothing anyway. I have a small rush job at present, some little drawings for School books so it's goodbye to Art for now.

Best regards to L. & the rest of your family.

25 Severn Street,
July 22, 1936

Thanks for your letter. I can't say that the summer has been very enjoyable so far. Too dry. We have had no rain for 32 days & the thermometer went to 110° in the shade for several days. On Saturday we had great excitement in the village. The hayfield to the north got on fire & swept down on the back fences and woodsheds.

The bells rang & called out the town, all the retired farmers & old maids came running with pails, sacks & brooms but were unable to stop the flames. Just in time the Richmond Hill, Lansing, & Maple fire engines arrived else most of the town would have gone. It will cost us $35 for each engine, $105 in all.

Things are quiet round the old Severn Valley. A.Y.J. in Europe & most of the others on vacation. I don't know what happens in the Art World. It's dreaming the summer hours away. I haven't done much work except to cut the hay etc. I have a new English rivet back scythe & man O man, does she cut. She walks right away from you. Half a million $ as W. says.

---

25 Severn Street,
1939

I thought I'd let you know that Fanny Bowes' house in Thornhill that you liked so much is for sale.

I think the price would be around $3000. It's a good buy as it's rented for $24.00. It's very well built as it was put up by old Jos. Mastin, the best builder in the neighbourhood.

I don't know the details but it's in the hands of an old Quaker neighbour, Jacob Reaman.

---

25 Severn Street, Toronto,
September 18, 1940

Glad to hear from you & the u.s. It makes one feel like moving over there.

Work is very scarce here & we're now in the midst of our 2nd War Loan which doesn't seem to be going very well. R.S. McLaughlin has taken another million but so far I haven't been able to follow his example. Lowrie was just in here also complaining of being hard up. Walter, however, has lots of work and plans to enlarge his shop.

Harvest here is still going on as it has rained all the time & the poor old farmers are up against it for fair, no help, terrible weather & worse prices. Grain has been out for weeks & is growing into a solid mat. Must be old Hitler's fault, everybody says. Potatoes also are poor in our section, we have an acre & none larger than golf balls.

My mother had a fall & broke her arm but seems to be mending OK. Took it out of splints yesterday. Bob Hunter has no work yet. His book is being printed so gives him something to think about.

Thornhill,
March 10, 1941

No pens available, all in the hands of ladies. Thanks for yours. Sorry you're feeling blue but the times are not very cheery, enough to make the rabbits bite & growl.

Charles Comfort is recovered. Lawren Jr. is taking 6 mos. training, something he doesn't seem to enjoy. In his absence Lowrie acts as deputy landlord & is very businesslike. A well known Englishman, Mr Wyndham Lewis, is in Lawren's studio. Suppose you've heard of Banting's end, too bad, but at least he won't do any more painting. I guess A.Y.J. felt badly. So much for Art news.

Work is very scarce here & I'm on the watch for a few cheap acres where I can starve to death quietly. There is a piece up in King Twp. for $450. There doesn't seem to be any immediate prospect of military activity for me so may as well have all the peace possible.

Yesterday I went to a very interesting sale. All the tools etc. of a local barn builder. Lots of fine things but so many people you couldn't get anywhere near. Also 800 books & everyone a Western. Funny to see some of the old fellows in fringed overcoats & maybe bags around their feet come out & climb in big new cars.

I haven't seen the Gray's Elegy you mention as I seldom go in Britnells' now but will take a look. About my own leaflets, I'll send you what I have on hand & perhaps you'll pass them on. No need to charge anything. They're all out of date anyhow. I meant to do one or two more (Great Horned Owls) but the war has put the brakes on. I haven't paid income taxes yet but my other taxes came to over $360, business, office, & sales tax. I see we're spending about $2000 a minute on the war. Not bad for population of 10 million.

My mother's hand is somewhat better but in general she doesn't seem too good.

Lots of foxes around this winter.

April 21, 1941

Thanks for letter. There's no special news from these parts. Our new tenant, Wyndham Lewis, has been making a portrait of J.S.McLean. I should tell you Mr Lewis says he considers you the best painter he's seen in these woods, better than Burchfield. Alec of course is down in P.Q. looking over the sway-backed plugs and sagging ridgepoles that he finds there. Lowrie acts as landlord & sells perfume & vases. In between time he dashes off an inspirational masterpiece or two. Hilter, Princess Elizabeth & myself have just celebrated our birthday. I have a shot of rheumatics to remind me that old age is creeping on. Makes heavy work difficult.

Mr Nash asks me to send a drawing or two but so far I haven't been able to make anything new. If you see him please tell him I'm trying to get something worth while.

Are you anywhere near Middlebury? I had some correspondence with the librarian there. They have a great collection of American stuff, the Abernathy Library. My mother is fairly well. Regards to all.

Another interesting outfit is the Stephen Daye Press at Brattleboro.

Thornhill,
August 15, 1943

Thanks for writing. I've often wondered how things were going with you. There's little change here. Everyone away just now,

A.Y.J. in Banff. My time is spent mostly in the fields as hands are so scarce even the poorest tools are welcome. I'm working with an old neighbour of 75 so have an easy time.

I hear now & then from Bob Hunter who is plugging along as a private in the U.S. army. He finds it hard work not being very strong, but says he can now handle various weapons. '*Grands*,' 'bazookas,' etc.

I don't suppose you would chance to hear of my old friend Thos. Hennell the writer & artist. I've been wondering if he's alive. He used to live at 'Orchard Cottage,' Ridley, Wrotham, Kent.

Crops are none too good in this section, some oats, barley etc. the poorest ever seen. Tiny shocks like toys scattered about the fields. Foxes and skunks are plentiful & deer are seen.

All keep fairly well here.

Best regards to any Canucks I know.

Thornhill,
October 28, 1943

Thanks for yours. Glad to hear of your doings also to hear that Hennell is OK. I was afraid he had got in the way of something, as he hadn't written. As to news from these parts I can't think of much, I seldom come in contact with the Art gang. A.Y.J. is out inspecting the Alaska highway. The old Studio Building is principally tenanted by strangers. Even Walter intends leaving. Bob Hunter was here. He has been discharged and looks pretty thin. He expects to get some job in Florida so I guess we'll seldom see him. I guess you heard that Lowrie got married to a Miss Buchan. Can't think of anything else.

We had a little snow & have the furnace lit though we get only 50% of last year's coal. However, I have about 2 ½ cords of wood all cut, split & inside. Wood is $20 a cord to buy. Owing to fuel shortage my mother plans to go to town but I'll stick it out here by the good old Quebec heater. I see enough of Toronto without sleeping there. As my namesake might say

What's Toronto to me
I never go to see
The Art Gallery,
Hart House, the museum
I never want to see 'em
Nor to hear Sir MacMillan
Reg. Stewart, Healy Willan
The Arts & Sciences
And all their appliances
Away with them, give us Thornhill.

September 21, 1955

I saw Will Ogilvie Monday & he told me Mark is married O& in the Hearst district. Please give him regards & goodwishes when you write.

Sorry to bother you at this busy time but I lent M. a couple of books by H.D. Thoreau, *Succession of Forest Trees*, & *The Maine Woods*. Doesn't matter about the first but I need *Maine Woods* for some Indian words & measurements of pointers. If you're ever in this district we'd be glad to see you or I might try & pick it up at your place. Better come up here & see the old place before it's submerged in the suburbs.

Thornhill,
May 1, 1957

Thanks for the prints. I'm glad to have them, especially Baker's old stake and rider fence.

The portraits are good likenesses too. I'll be looking forward to seeing the slides.

I've not seen or heard anything of Will but he must be busy on his farm. I hope it will work out well. Also hope L. is recovered.

CHAPTER VI

Letters to Ray Nash

March 17, 1941

Thanks for your letter. I would be glad to submit something for your *Quarterly.* Perhaps you will tell me the size & type of drawing you would like, that is if your colleagues feel I could provide something suitable.

    I haven't much experience in print making as my work has been mostly pen drawing for zinc blocks.

In hunting through the bookcase I found another Woodcut book now out of print which I'm sending.

May 7, 1941

I'm sending you a couple of drawings which you may be able to use. I hoped to make something special but there's so much to be done on the land at this time of year.

RAY NASH is a retired professor of art. He taught at Dartmouth College for thirty years, courses called *Prints and Printing* and *The Art of the Book.* His morning lectures, in which his students could handle his collection of prints and fine books, provided the historical background of book design, printing, and illustration; his afternoon workshop followed up with actual practice in setting type, printing woodblocks, making engravings or etchings, handling tools, paper, and presses. He was an editor of the magazine *Print,* and also of PAGA (Printing and Graphic Arts). For fifty years he has had a farm in Vermont, where he occasionally takes a few students for his summer workshop. He is the author of *Calligraphy and Printing in the 15th Century* (1940, 1964), *Durer's 1511 Drawing of a Press and Printer* (1947), *Printing as an Art* (1955), *American Writing Masters and Copybooks* (1959), and *American Penmanship* (1969).

So far I haven't been able to see a copy of *Print* so haven't attempted a cover design but perhaps later I might be able to do so. I'm enclosing a cover for a local catalogue which shows the type of thing I had in mind.

The other drawings have never been reproduced.

Some of the drawings I would like returned if possible.

August 21, 1941

I'm sending you a rough suggestion for the cover of *Print*. It has

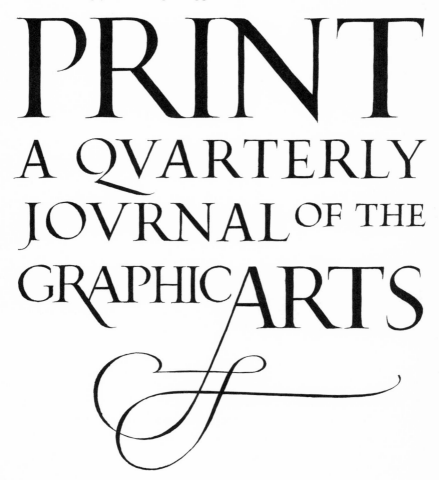

nothing much to recommend it except the possible dignity of the letter forms, which I could try to do as well as I could.

After such delay on my part I won't be disappointed if you are unable to use it.

September 29, 1941

I'm very pleased to hear that I can go ahead with a design for *Print* & will do my best to make something worthwhile. . . . As my health hasn't been so good my work has gone slowly but I will send the working drawings before long.

I'm glad you are a Thoreau MacDonald enthusiast, especially as you're almost the only one I ever heard of. If you have not seen them I would like to send you copies of 2 or 3 books such as *Maria Chapdelaine* & *West by East*. Perhaps you will let me know if you have them down there.

---

25 Severn Street,
Toronto, October 31

I'm sending a copy of *Maria Chapdelaine*. No need to return it. The other books I mentioned are less interesting, so I didn't include them.

I guess the old Woodchuck Press will remain dormant during the war. It had a number of things in mind but they will have to wait . 'Wild Animals of Vaughan Township' was one, with lithographs.

December 8, 1942

Many thanks for your letters & cards. I'm sorry all my moose drawings are away in a show & won't be available in time for Christmas, otherwise I'd have been very glad to send you the one you liked.

Your farm looks a mighty nice place. Carl Schaefer told me something about it.

I like Mr Frost's poems too, & would certainly feel honoured to have him look at anything of mine. I will ask the publisher to send on a few copies of Hunter's book.

Thornhill,
December 29, 1942

Unless floods or blizzards prevent I will be in Toronto tomorrow & send the moose & other drawings to you & hope you'll not be disappointed in them.

I noted the overlapping of correspondence; it's nice to have one's work appreciated in such a way. It seldom happens.

Thanks for your greeting card with the bit of 16th century printing.

Best wishes for the New Year to you & Mrs Nash.

Box 197,
Thornhill, Ontario,
Canada, October 6, 1943

How are you? Dr Pierce of Toronto showed me a copy of *Print* with some lettering by myself (none to good). It's an honour for a hick like myself to contribute to such a distinguished journal & I want to thank you for your kind words in the list of contributors.

But I expect my father's turning in his grave at being called an 'English oil painter' for he was passionately Canadian & nationalistic. His ancestors had been in America since 1630 & in Canada since about 1780.

I wish you could have heard his lectures on printing & book production. However that's enough bragging.

I was mighty interested to hear about *Print* being edited on a farm & would like to help by subscribing but finances won't stand it now. If there's any kind of work I could do that would be useful I would like to contribute it free. But I guess it's mainly financial help that's necessary.

I have been glad to hear from a friend of yours, Henry Beston in Maine. He sent me some printing by you, the *Squawberry.*

January 21, 1944

The little writing book came safely. I certainly appreciate it. It's a fine job & apart from all the research is so nicely printed & pleasant to handle. I have been on the lookout for local examples but so far haven't found anything old enough to have any interest. Some

121

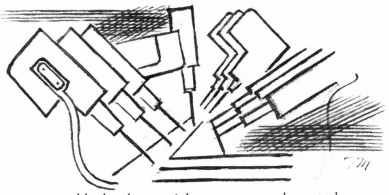

years ago an old school master's house was torn down & there were some good things destroyed. While on the subject of writing I fear mine is even worse than usual, having squashed a finger while handling logs. If it's handy & if you have any proofs of the Dartmouth Press mark I made for you I would like a copy for record. Please don't go to any trouble.

February 12, 1944

Many thanks for sending me the book.* I'm glad to have it as an example of printing. I was rather sorry to see the lettering left off the mark as I thought it the best part. The book just arrived else I'd have written sooner.

    Must now get in wood for the night. Again thanks & best regards.

If there's anything you need from Canada I'd be glad to try to get it.

* *Motivation And Visual Factors*

May 23, 1944

Thanks for your kind letter. I appreciate it. The cuts you speak of are so old that I'm rather ashamed of them. . . . I hoped to make better ones but have had other things to do & lately haven't felt up to much.

For a long time I've thought of drawing something to accompany one or two of Mr Frost's poems, such as the one called (if I remember right) 'Stopping By Woods On a Snowy Evening.' My father was an admirer of Mr Frost's work. I wonder if I sent you a copy of *West by East* which has some of that type of drawings? Please let me know as I'd like you to see it though it has many faults.

I would very much like to show some work at your college if I had enough good stuff. However, I've found it very hard to send things back & forth over the border. I'll see what's on hand. Thanks again.

May 29, 1944

Many thanks for your letter & proofs of the seal drawings. I felt mighty honoured to be mentioned near Mr Dwiggins.

I'm sending a copy of *West by East,* unfortunately not new as it's out of print. I didn't like to send it before on account of the poor lettering of the title page & some other faults. It should be all done over.

I forgot to say that most of those old 'woodcuts' are only linoleum. If this is any use for your purpose I'd gladly send them. Most are not even type-high.

June 8, 1944

I'm sending you a few old cuts, mostly junk I'm afraid. I find many of them are brittle, split & not worth sending, so had to put in a few zincs to fill up. Could send more zincs if they're any use to you. . . .

WEST
by EAST
& OTHER POEMS BY
J·E·H·MACDONALD

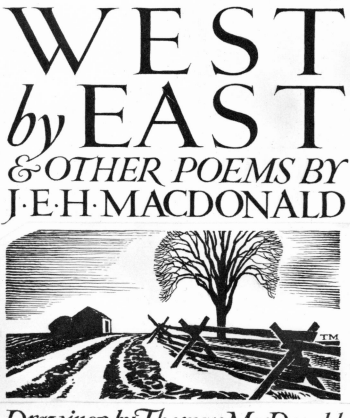

Drawings by Thoreau MacDonald

WEST BY EAST

November 10, 1944

I'm glad to hear from you again for I began to fear I might have
been too crabby in refusing your good invitation to Hanover. I'll
do all my best to make a new drawing though I may have to delay it
a week as I'm struggling with a few such problems already delayed
too long. If I don't hear from you I'll suppose this OK.

April 30, 1945

I'm sending you a drawing of the 1776 U.S. seal. I can't be sure of all
the details & I guess any heraldic expert would get a laugh from it.
You'll notice I put in a sickle to represent farming. It fits in better
than grain & I guess is just as good a symbol for the purpose. I
haven't been able to do anything yet for the Audubon Society.
When it's handy for you let me know size & any preferred subjects.
Also could you photostat copies if I couldn't always send original
drawings.

THOREAU
MᴬᶜDONALD
DESIGNER

25 Severn St.
Toronto, Canada

Dear Mr. Nash —
I'm sending the working drawing for
PRINT & hope its good enough. Its not my
first attempt which is the reason I've been so
slow: I have been rather shaky & of course
you need to be feeling well to do good lettering.
I should have drawn it on card the proper
size but Strathmore is very scarce.

Best regards,

Thoreau MacDonald

May 11, 1945

As I don't know much of the technicalities of Heraldry I'm afraid
that sketch I sent was only a layout of the haziest sort. According
to the books, quarterings of 4 are numbered thus . . . so I suppose
6 would be. . . . Apparently they are still called quarterings even
when the divisions number 28. I only put them down at random &
the same with those escutcheons bearing the initials of the States

but I think No 1, N.H. would be as you say under the Eye of the Almighty & so on clockwise. I could attempt a drawing of it especially as you say there's no hurry.

About the N.H. Audubon Bulletin, for such a worthy object I'd be glad to contribute drawings *free.* Just let me know the size & when to go ahead. In the meantime I'll keep it in mind & see if I've anything suitable at hand.

I'm glad to hear Mr Frost likes that drawing.

Later I see the heraldic authority Fox-Davies says you may have any number of quarterings on a shield & they are counted from dexter to sinister beginning with the top row & so on. He also says 'they are done to accident & mean practically nothing.'

September 25, 1945

How are you? I wonder if you ever rec'd an attempt at a *Print* cover I sent you. I also have a few drawings for the Audubon Society should they need them.

25 Severn Street,
Toronto 5, March 8, 1948

Thanks for letter & Mr Rice's prints. The woodcut is a beautiful impression. I'm glad to see it as I find myself getting careless with such things. If you can give away any copies of the hunting leaflet let me know as unfortunately I have *hundreds*. I thought perhaps the drawings for it might be of some use so am sending them, also the pencil layouts. I make the roughest kind of sketch on waste paper (then I'm not scared of spoiling it). These almost subconscious scribblings often have what I want. Then trace them with pencil onto good stuff & go ahead. However, I guess there's nothing new in this. I'm enclosing a few other odds & ends.

I have some other sets of illustrations if you ever need any. *Mountain Cloud. Longhouse Nest.* etc.

April 20, 1948

Thanks for yours of 18th. I'm glad if you get any good out of the drawings. I thought after perhaps you had copies of the *Mountain Cloud* drawings. I didn't send the book as it has some pretty bad spots, not altogether my fault. I'd be glad if the Beston book goes through but so far I've heard nothing of it.

June 16, 1948

Thanks for the Cowles sheet. It's a success & the titles look interesting.

I'm having a struggle with Henry Beston's illustrations as it's a race against time. Rineharts want everything by July 6. I'd like to give it more time & thought & on top of that haying is coming on. As Rineharts are paying little for the 46 drawings I thought of specifying that the originals go to your department if H.B. approves. I have 24 done so far.

September 22, 1948

I'll be glad to have a try at Mount Mansfield. It's certainly a fine piece of rock & the photo itself would be hard to improve on. However, I'll keep in mind what you say & try to send something in a few days. I'm just at the end of another Rinehart book, *The Mackenzie*, for the Rivers of America set. Henry Beston seemed to think he'd like to have those drawings for his book himself so I thought maybe you might take this Mackenzie art instead, if Rineharts don't keep them. Anyhow I'll try to send Mt Mansfield for your approval soon.

December 12, 1948

Thanks for the sample copy of *Print*. I'm sorry you had to use that old lettering; not very good. I'd be glad to submit a design *gratis* any time.

May 19, 1949

. . . I got rid of 40 pounds of zinc blocks. With some hesitation I'm sending the remainder as I can't think what use it can be.

Lino blocks make good fuel but it's too hot just now.

For the present I've been unable to find a workplace; am a misplaced person.

August 3, 1949,
Thornhill

Enclosed are a couple of versions of the bell tower. In the larger one the sky tone could be masked off & might look better.

We surely appreciated your visit though after I remembered a good many things I meant to ask & show you.

January 4, 1950

Thanks for the Dartmouth Calendar. I almost feel as if I'd been to College. Sorry I had nothing suitable at Christmas for you. I've been trying to get a publisher for our conversation book. Just lost my cat from pneumonia, a painful memory. Hope your old dog continues well.

January 12, 1950

I wasn't worried about the fox. . . .

    I'm sorry Rineharts didn't send you all the Mackenzie drawings. The author got the others for what reason I know not. I'm trying to forget the book. Bad printing keeps me awake nights. But I have little connection with the graphic arts these days. I miss my cat more than art. I'm like the man in Hardy's poem — By the Roman Grave-mounds.

March 21, 1950

Please tell Mr Stinehour I'll look forward to seeing his first publication. He's welcome to anything I've made or have. Maybe when he gets started we may pull off something. At present the poor old Woodchuck is laying low, scared by the realistic developments.

    Let me know if there's anything I can do for the North Country Press.

June 14, 1950

Many thanks to you & Stinehour for the booklets. It makes a person feel pretty important to see one's feeble scratching *tipped down.* If some time you could send one extra copy it would be appreciated by a Toronto collector. Any time will do. I haven't succeeded in getting our natural resources book printed or I'd send one. All publishers seem scared of the subject.

Regards to all, also the North Country Press.

This writing looks bad compared to your script but I've just inscribed 170 Dental Diplomas, also a piece of tractor flew off & hit me in the eye.

February 16, 1951

While time remains I hope to pint about 60 or 70 drawings, mostly new. I plan to produce them cheaply by offset, paper covers, stapled together. What I want to bother you about is this. As the *Northern Farm* drawings were so miserably printed I thought to include a few of them handy. I've listed them on the back of this card. There's no hurry. I'll call the drawings *Fields & Woods* or *Woods & Fields* & will get a lot of things off my mind.

From *Northern Farm:*

page 85	chapter XVI
153	XXVIII
171	XXXII
239	XLV
53	X
63	XII

239 ? 85 are the best; doesn't matter about the rest. Sorry to give this trouble but will send a copy of the book.

February 24, 1951

Sorry to have bothered you about those drawings but anyhow perhaps it's better to use only unpublished stuff. I never hear from Henry Beston, maybe I hurt his feelings in some way.

Never had any success with the forestry book, even tried English publishers. Market's too limited.

Carl Schaefer called Thursday, spoke of you. We went to look at some muskeg which he drew while I looked for muskrats.

[?]

I'm sending one of the foxes, not a first rate drawing unfortunately. I thought the other too much a naturalist's study. I hardly ever make them now, doing field work in summer & now commercial stuff of the poorest kind. As I said just send me one of your books. . . .

Let me know if you don't care for this one & I'll make something else.

May 26, [?]

I've just received a handsome copy of Direct Advertising which I guess I owe to you. I'm looking forward to reading your article on Dwiggins in there. I'm always learning from him.

I'm just starting on Henry Beston's book & I hope I can make a good job of it. For some reason I find it harder & harder to do good work.

CHAPTER VII

Letters to Lorne Pierce

25 Severn Street,
[Thursday, June 30, 1933]

I have the ms and your note. I'm glad you approve the selection.

I haven't thought much about the name but unless it is simply called 'Poems by J.E.H. MacD.,' I thought perhaps something like 'From Canada' or 'In Ontario.' My father would like something nationalistic & unsentimental. I think too it would be good to date them. I think the cost should certainly not exceed $1.50 per copy. A well designed book can be as cheap as any. I would like to use Caslon type throughout, with some small cuts & a jacket in colour.

Thank you for the work on Dr Burt's book.

LORNE PIERCE, editor of The Ryerson Press from 1920 to 1960, was greatly responsible for the development of arts and letters in Canada during the time that Thoreau knew him. He edited *The Makers of Canadian Literature* (13 vols.) and the Ryerson Poetry Chap-Books. He wrote monographs about authors such as Bliss Carman and Marjorie Pickthall, and in 1940 and 1942 wrote 'J.E.H. MacDonald: a Postscript' and 'Thoreau MacDonald' respectively.

25 Severn Street,
September 11, 1933

I have my father's verses ready & have made a number of small drawings. I think it would be well to have proofs & page them up in order to see what spaces there will be before going further.

I haven't tried to illustrate the poems especially but only to accompany them as harmoniously as I could.

My father told me last summer — 'Just put a few things like that in,' and he pointed to the cat sleeping under the berry bushes. About 5½ x 8 inches would be the best size or as near that as possible. I would like the type and layout to be the same as the 'Village & Fields' booklet with one or two small changes. The jacket can be simple & in one colour, the binding dark green with a small blind stamped title. The title-page might be best set in the same type (Caslon o.s.) as the text with a vignette, or else I can draw the whole thing. Whenever you wish I can bring the copy down with directions for the typesetting. There are 30 poems.

Monday, [?], 1937

Sorry to have been so slow with these layouts.

I'd suggest using the same type as in the other series if possible. The margins might be a little wider as indicated, & the paper 'Plainfield Offset Ivory' a pleasant colour.

The cover layout would be repeated as a title-page.

It seems to be the one marked x is better than the others.

If you wish me to come down I can do so any time.

[?], 1937

I'm sorry to have been so slow with this but have had tooth trouble.

The paper you gave me seems slightly lighter in colour than the Mayfair Brown of which I attach a sample. If this is so I think it would be best to use the Mayfair Brown.

[?], 1937

Only when I got *The Bookman* today I remembered that I didn't give you a drawing for it.

I had this one ready but with teeth & other things forgot to deliver it. I'm awfully sorry.

The title is 'The Barnyard.'

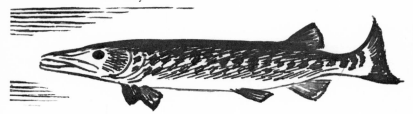

25 Severn Street,
Tuesday, [?], 1937

Thank you for sending M. Boulanger's letter about 'W. by E.'

I suppose it would be good to have a French edition if it was done well. I would be very pleased to see one made. The drawings leave much to be desired & must be improved some day.

If there are copies for sale I would like to buy a couple. I think those poems will some time be a landmark in the expanse of Canadian literature.

They seem to wear well.

I hope you feel well these days.

[?], 1937

In case you are not in I write to say that I think 'The Elements' print would look best mounted on a dark paper as shown in this little layout. I think white paper kills a colour repro. It could have a narrow black & gold frame printed around it.

The size would be 8 x 10½".

I should have made the layout full size but lacked the paper. It is 'Mayfair Brown,' a very good colour I think.

25 Severn Street,
Monday, [?], 1937

These are the notes on my father I spoke of, I hope they will be some help. As you say, the publication will be kept quiet at present. Let me know if the sketch you got is not satisfactory in your house.

---

25 Severn Street,
Wednesday, [November 18, 1937]

Thanks for cheque and note.

Certainly Hennell's poems are strange to me. But in some parts I find those unexpected turns & touches so like reality that make me think they have some kind of genius in them.

His 'Change in the Farm' is a wonderful book. I enclose a copy of his letter.

Box 197,
Thornhill, Monday
[June 28, 1938]

I haven't sent you a drawing as I thought you might be using the caricature of 'The Critics.' I can let you have another of course & perhaps will call with it if you would not be tired by a call.

I thought the log house looked fairly well though thinly printed.

About the cover, of course I didn't want anything for the drawing so don't think about that expense. The only cost would be the cut.

I hoped you would be quite well by now, sorry you are not so good.

25 Severn Street
Thursday, [March 10, 1939]

This *Colophon* was overlooked when I delivered the others. It may
be useful somewhere. . . .
    If it's convenient might I get the last *Bookman* drawing
(Goshawk).

---

25 Severn Street,
Toronto, Monday, [?]

Thanks for yours of July 8. I find I forgot to put a note in with the
Charlesworth clipping. Times have changed since then.
    I thought that the drawings for *The Bookman* might be called
'Old Ontario' or 'Scenes of Country Life.'
    I'm afraid my mother will never make a book alone but
perhaps her material can be combined with Hunter's to round it
out somewhat.
    I hope you have a good holiday.

---

25 Severn Street,
Wednesday, [August 2, 1939]

Bob Hunter has set me his book on my father & wishes me to speak
to you regarding its publication this year.
    I think he has improved it considerably.
    Perhaps you will let me know if you intend going ahead &
then I will try to improve my part of it & perhaps the layout,
illustrations, etc. It seems to me well worth while.
    Thornhill remains about the same. I hear that Mazo de
LaRoche is moving into the neighbourhood.
    I hope you are well.

Thornhill, Wednesday, [?], 1940

After looking up my available drawings & thinking over the problems concerned I would really far rather not put on the Gallery exhibit this fall. I'm sorry that you have had so much trouble over it already. But I do appreciate your efforts on my behalf, even though I feel *I must decline* it for the present. Later I may ask Mr Laing to show the birds & animals & in the meantime I will prepare my father's early work.

I have a note from Hunter saying he is rewriting his article on the lines you suggested. Whatever faults it may have I can think of no one to do it better.

Thursday, [?], 1940

Here is a try at the note for Hunter's book.

Perhaps it should be longer but I'm a poor hand at such things. I hope you approve it. I will have the layout for 'The Elements' in a day or so.

25 Severn Street, Toronto,
Thursday, February 9, 1940

Bob Hunter tells me you plan to print his book shortly and I've been wondering if you would let me design the Jacket, title-page, etc.

I have thought about it considerably and have made some layouts. I would certainly appreciate it very much if you could leave the design of the book to me and would try to make a good job in harmony with the Morrice volume. Of course I wouldn't charge anything for the work.

I hope you keep well.

25 Severn Street,
Tuesday, [September 5, 1940]

I enclose a cover stamp for Hunter's Book. The oak leaf has a special significance. I'd rather not put any lettering on the cover.

I'm sorry the book is causing you so much work & worry. If you would allow me I would be glad to look after the printing details. Just let me see the printers & you need not think of it again.

As Mr Laing says, 2 of the pictures reproduced have been sold to R.S. McLaughlin. I suppose their catalogue references should be changed.

I hope I told you that any work I do is *gratis*.

Tuesday, [?], 1940

Sorry to bother you but it seems a pity to discard the jacket when the drawings & zincs are all made.

Last time I was in, Mr Hasselman told me they were printing it. It's one of the best parts of the book, more important than the gold stamping which is only a luxury.

To save money I thought to use the first rejected printing of 'Elements.' It would look OK there.

I gave the printer careful layouts with all measurements, etc.

Monday, [?], 1940

I'm very sorry I wasn't home when you came yesterday, but I appreciate your call just the same.

Some of the proofs of *the Forum* cuts are disappointing. I didn't realize there were so many of my own & very poor ones too. They had better be returned to Dent's as useless. I've marked the titles on any that are good.

Thanks for letting me see Gagnon's book. I will return it in a few days. At present I'm out on part time.

---

25 Severn Street,
Thursday, [?], 1940

I have marked about 10 of these which I thought might receive copies of your Postcript. Some of the 10 might also be eliminated if you think so.

[?], 1941

I have retouched Dr Barbeau's photoprint slightly & think Brigden can make a good zinc from it. M. Barbeau will be pleased to have it used as he planned & it should make a fair cover.

Monday, [?], 1941

Here are a couple of colour layouts for Dr Barbeau's booklet. I don't think it really necessary to vary the colours as every book will have a different design on it. Unless good colour inks are used it's better to stick to black on different cover stocks.

I suggest adding a couple of rules as shown to tie it together better.

On the spine I would just use all one size of type but the author & publisher set in Italics. I thought the booklets were to be saddle-stitched & if so no spine would be possible.

I will return the copy of *Print* soon.

Friday, [February 9, 1942]

Thanks for the check, received today. The warden of Hart House tells me you have been kind enough to speak about my drawings over there. I hope it won't be too much trouble.

I didn't suggest your name to the warden as I thought it might add to your work.

I'm sorry there are only a few of the 50 odd drawings made for 'Maria Chapdelaine' over there but hadn't room.

I thought you might be interested in this old 3 colour woodcut, never before printed.

---

25 Severn Street,
[March 6, 1942]

Many thanks for the booklet. It's a theme that needs harping on these days for it's hard to see what's ahead for Canada whatever the outcome of the war.

Though Canadians are patriotic enough, in one way the majority don't seem to care much about their country as a land, a home.

A lot of them would sell the last acre if they could get enough to live in Bermuda or Florida. As a piece of land our country is fast deteriorating & nobody seems to care.

I thought the type & printing of your booklet were very good. The type is an unusually nice face.

Thursday, [?], 1942

Here are a couple of layouts for the Fiction Award. It woul cost about $15.00 to draw it in hand lettering so perhaps would be more economical to set it in type. The paper should be about 10 x 12″.

I hope you keep well.

Thursday, [?], 1942

Thanks for letting me read the essay. It's hard for me to give any opinion on such a personal subject but it makes one feel like working so it must be good.

Mr Jefferys' letter is very encouraging too as I have great respect for him & his opinions.

Mr Flemington sent a sample of paper for the Fiction Award which seems very nice.

Monday, [?], 1942

I hope the enclosed imprint is more what you had in mind. I wouldn't reduce it too much, perhaps about 1½″.

Several people have spoken to me about your paper.

I forgot to say that it might be well to put 'The Ryerson Press etc.' under the design of the Chapbook cover, which was the reason I didn't make it deeper.

May 22, 1942

Thanks for your letter of yesterday. No need to thank me as the presentation meant no sacrifice on my part.

I sent you yesterday two designs for marks & enclosed the drawing of A.Y.J. which I'd be glad to have you keep if you like it. I don't suppose it would offend A.Y.J.

25 Severn Street,
Friday, [?], 1942

I'm returning Hunter's monograph and list of illustrations. It will only be necessary to make 3 or 4 new cuts.

I have taken the liberty of writing a few remarks on Hunter's mss not that they need be listened to. I hope he may come here this summer & we can talk it over. I rather dread the publicity but I suppose it won't amount to much.

For the 'Canadian Spokesman' a drawn cover design seems unnecessary & I'd suggest a Caslon type-set title like the enclosed layout. For Queens I could gather about 50 drawings that would be representative without repetition. They would include 'Maria Chapdelaine' & might fill 4 large frames.

Tuesday, [?], 1942

This list of cuts shows those that should be in the book. I can always provide more if necessary. My object has been to avoid making new cuts as far as possible.

The list of books is a hard problem as there are so many now forgotten. I would advise leaving it out entirely as it's impossible to make it complete or accurate.

I enclose a note from Scott Carter you may like to read.

Illustrations for *T. MacD* by E.R. Hunter
Those marked X require new cuts. 6 or 7 new cuts will be necessary.

Early lino cut	Mapleleaf Gate
Hunter's Cabin X	The Goshawk
Pioneer Graves	Industrious Bear
House at Thornhill X	*'Maria Chapdelaine'* X
Year on the Farm (2 or 3)	*C.N.E. catalogue* '39 X
Old Gate (last in book)	*Woodshed Door* X (not necessary)
Rapids at Night X	*Moose* X (halftone)
The Lane	*The Lane II* X

This makes 17. I can supply as many more as there may be space for. The cover & frontis are already decided & OK'd by Hunter. 'Henri Julien' contains 25 cuts.

Thursday, [?], 1942

Enclosed is a layout for Mr Birney's Poem, I would use type for the spine. To save money we could use the mountain cut on buff paper which I made for you some time ago & perhaps you still have the block.

'The Iceberg' book has some faults, the awful type in the halftitle & the little whale in the lower right corner. He should have been centered.

It will cost very little to make drawings for *David* etc.

THE ICEBERG & OTHER POEMS BY C.G.D. ROBERTS Ryerson

[?], 1942

I'm returning these proofs with 5 suggested changes.

THE
ICEBERG
AND OTHER POEMS BY
CHARLES G·D·ROBERTS

TORONTO The RYERSON PRESS 1934

FOR TITLE PAGE
4½"

I would much rather leave out any galleries having drawings if you don't mind.

Changes on —
Cover
title page
p. 5
p. 30-31
p. 38-39

The ICEBERG & OTHER POEMS
CHARLES G. D. ROBERTS

25 Severn Street,
Friday, [?], 1942

My mother & I feel that it's not right to expect you to buy land at Thornhill when you are settled at York Mills & have so many demands on you already. Please don't think of it any more. Later on I may be able to do more myself & we have the Elm anyway.

As you like that apple tree sketch I enclose a similar one. Please accept it with sincere regards.

Tuesday, [?], 1942

There hardly seems a need for any hand work on this book unless you wish to use a portrait.

I hope the printer won't mind using fairly large type, preferably the monotype Caslon. The colophon also should be a good size.

25 Severn Street,
Wednesday, [?], 1942

Since talking with you I've heard one or two things re Group of Seven that make me hesitate about going further on plates etc. A.Y. Jackson tells me the National Gallery is sponsoring a history of the subject to be published in England & which he thinks should make all else superfluous. It will appear this spring. Then I notice Macmillans have brought out a history of Canadian Art which seems to overlap Colgates'. This makes me wonder if we would be justified in spending money on halftones which will cost quite a bit. It seems as though Canadian Art may be overdone. I won't go further before hearing from you.

25 Severn Street,
Tuesday, [?], 1942

Thanks for the Poetry Chapbook. I think it's an improvement on the old design. The mountains, tree & sky are much better.

I have gathered up my available drawings but apart from the sets such as 'Maria Chapdelaine,' 'Year on the Farm,' 'Gates,' etc. I have only about 30.

Perhaps you will look them over when you have time.

[?], 1942

Here are suggestions for *A Canadian People,* a very necessary book. I'm not sure whether you mean to have it in boards or paper. If you would like a drawing on the Jacket I have one or two that might be adapted.

What a pity the printer spoiled the *Long Sault* with that awful looking half-title. It should have been in 12 or 10 point caps. It would be wonderful if they could get rid of that terrible type & get some good faces. However enough complaints for today.

I hope you feel better.

I'll return *Print* very soon, am reading it.

Wednesday, [?], 1942

These are the dimensions you gave me for the little table or stand. If you like its looks we had better try to start Walter at it directly.

Mr Colgate came in & says he is worried about the layout of his book. He feels that as the designer I should look after it better.

I hope the title page will be OK. Perhaps I could see proofs some time.

Friday, [?], 1943

Dear Mr Flemington,*

Mr Colgate brought in this Jacket & I'm sorry to say it looks pretty terrible. I hope it won't be too late to rectify the worst features &

* Frank Flemington worked for many years at the Ryerson Press.

have marked some of them. The layout I supplied was quite differ-ent but I suppose it has been lost by now. I'm enclosing one which indicates our original intentions.

If neither of the 2 colours specified is available we'll have to get something else, certainly not the dreary raw liver tent of this proof.

The whole design must be moved over & up & some blurb added underneath to lengthen it. I'm sorry to make trouble but such a thing as this would be fatal. I would like to see a proof if I could & would go down any time.

---

25 Severn Street,
March 24, 1943

Thanks for the note & I'm very glad if you think the G. of 7 outline passable. There's quite a lot of stuffing to do yet but I suppose another thousand words won't hurt.

I'm hoping to have a layout ready for the Lampman poems in a day or so.

---

25 Severn Street,
Wednesday, [?], 1943

Dear Mr Flemington,

Mr Colgate has just been here re the divisions of his book. So far as appearances go it seems OK to stick to the original plan & it may make it easier to read.

About the initial letters of the chapters, I forgot how they were to be as it's so long since I made the layout. I think they should be either like E.R. Hunter's *J.E.H.MacD.* or like the *Maria Chapdelaine*.

Please tell Dr Pierce that Mr John Russel, the painter of C.G.D. Roberts' portrait is neither R.C.A. nor A.R.C.A. He belongs to no art bodies.

NO GOOD

layout OK but use CASLON OLDSTYLE as specified
long ago- NOT Caslon Bold. RULES too heavy. Use Hairline or ½ pt.

WILLIAM COLGATE

CANADIAN ART

ITS ORIGIN AND DEVELOPMENT

1820 - 1940

Introduction by C. W. Jefferys, R.C.A., LL.D.

The Ryerson Press - Toronto

Dear Mr. Flemington —
Seems to be wrong type again. I see no change except in the numerals &
Lord knows what they are. If they could use Caslon Old Style throughout &
light rules, then the layout would be OK. Please try to get them to do so & let me
know how you make out. Sorry to delay things.
— T.M.
Perhaps I had better draw it, might be cheaper. If so please return me this.

CANADIAN ART its origin & development

BY WILLIAM COLGATE

With a foreword by C. W. Jefferys, LL.D.
R.C.A.

Toronto · The Ryerson Press · 1943

CANADIAN ART *its origin & development*

BY WILLIAM COLGATE

with a foreword by C.W. Jefferys, R.C.A., LL.D.

TORONTO · THE RYERSON PRESS

4⅞" ✱

Please return to F. Macdonald, 25 Severn St. toronto

Friday, [?], 1943

This seems far, far better. If the rest of the book turns out as well, all should be OK.

I thought perhaps Dr Jefferys' words should be in quotation marks.

I hope you feel all right.

Thursday, [?], 1943

After thinking about those cheap pocket books most of last night it seems to me perhaps *Thunderbird* is rather an awkward mouthful especially as others have some prior claim on it. What do you think about *Falcon books*? Anyhow here are a few layouts including one for the cover. The colours could be varied carefully, & the titles drawn by hand. Garamond would be fine for the text.

I hope your weekend will be restful.

Monday, [?], 1943

Thanks for sending this proof. I've pencilled on a couple of suggestions. I'd set the title entirely in small caps & move up closer to cut. Please don't put my name on as initials are so big.

Inside, cut out the fancy O & use same caps. as in other words.

Centre names under greeting.

I think the falcon books have possibilities & will try & work out some better masks. Perhaps the *Village of Viger* might be published in that form.

In the Village of Viger

DUNCAN CAMPBELL SCOTT

[?], 1943

For the Jacket & Cover of Mrs Livesay's poems I'd suggest *Velvalur Apricot* if available. Otherwise an India or Gold. It seemed to me that the book paper of *David* was too soft, I mean the page stock. Something smoother & firmer would be better I think.

I'm returning the notes re Group of 7 with a few changes. Also enclose an account.

Tuesday, [?], 1943

Dear Mr Flemington,

Don't like to bother Dr Pierce so I thought I'd let you know that Mr Colgate would like a layout like the enclosed for his Jefferys' book.

I told him I thought all cuts are made but promised to send it along anyhow.

**THOREAU
MacDONALD
DESIGNER**

Monday

Dear Dr. Pierce —

After thinking over the drawing for your card I decided to do it all over in a rather different medium. I think it's a lot better. The other looked too scratchy & wiry. It will need to be printed on a fairly smooth stock like Mayfair or Plainfield Offset.

About the books, I only felt it looked a bit ostentatious to have my name on something that I had taken only a small part in.

As to the types it's hard to explain but it's like this in R for instance —

$$R_1 \quad R_2$$

1 is a common R used by Ryerson & you see what a sloppy form it has compared to the less degraded example 2. However, I guess hardly one in eleven million would notice it so probably our worry is superfluous. Sometime when I'm less lazy I want to draw some variations in Roman letters. Thoreau

DAY & NIGHT
Poems by Dorothy Livesay
THE RYERSON PRESS · TORONTO

DAVID

and other Poems by

EARLE BIRNEY

The Ryerson Press . Toronto
1942

WILLIAM COLGATE

CHARLES WILLIAM
JEFFERYS
Illustrator, Painter, Historian

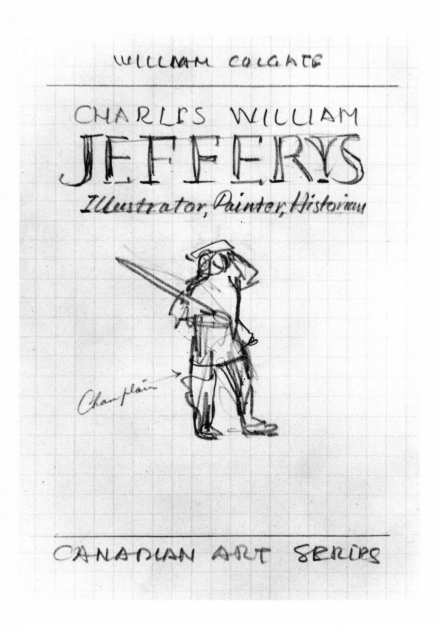

Champlain

CANADIAN ART SERIES

25 Severn Street,
August 31, 1943

Dear Mr Flemington,

Mr Colgate was here & is worried about one or two points in his
book, mainly *the Running Heads.*
   I think myself that it would be better to drop them altogether
rather than repeat *Canadian Art* on every page. That is if it won't
make too much trouble. Perhaps some time I could see some
proofs, also title page etc.

February 9, 1945

I'm much relieved to hear another lot of the Group of 7 is to be
made. It has been an awful worry as it's a fine piece of work gone
wrong. I didn't mean to belittle Jackson's note on Walter but the
old man couldn't be shown in such black & white simplicity. He
was a combination of tones, talking communism yet ever trying to
be a capitalist & individualist. He worshipped Russia yet knew he
could never live there, wouldn't take orders from anyone.
   He was always talking of what he called 'classical warfare' but
at the end it was to Russians of the old type that he felt closest. He
had no faith in any political system, 'nobody honest only the
animals.' He was shrewd & could make close deals but would work
free for poor folks. An interesting type & a genius.
   I hope the Group of 7 turns out well this time.

April 10, 1945

I've just read *A Canadian People.* It's great stuff, especially the last
2 chapters. If only it will sink in. Let's hope so.

25 Severn Street,
October 9, 1945

Dear Mr Flemington,

Sorry to bother you especially as I suppose it's out of your department. I note I'm supposed to get a statement re *Group of Seven* in
September. I've been wondering about it because I hope that miserable 2nd printing won't be allowed to go out.

That would be *the last straw that capped the vortex* & I would
feel compelled to make a public protest. I'd appreciate anything
you could do.

[?], 1945

I think best to go ahead with this only changing the *Colophon* to
the one indicated. I'm writing Dr Scott & hope to convince him
this is the best, everything considered.

(T.M. says he has heard from D.C.S. who says he is sure we have
done our best. He (T.M.) says to go ahead. L.P.)

---

25 Severn Street,
Tuesday, [?]

Thanks for the invitation to your garden party but I expect you
won't be surprised if you don't see me there. As I get older &
crabbier I seem more & more unsuited to any social life. However,
I appreciate being asked & hope you have good weather & feel well.

February 19, 1946

Miss Bivikova found Muriel looking much better. She is able to get up in afternoons, but doesn't think of returning to School before Spring. I don't know whether she would be wise to take it up again. Miss B. suggested she study with her as she has some private students. It would be free of course.

However, time enough to see about that later. Unfortunately Sister Dorcas was also laid up so couldn't give a report.

February 25, 1947

I'm sorry to bother you but I've been foolish enough to promise to lend some hawk pictures to the Zoological Dept. of the Museum. Would it be possible to borrow one or both of those you have for a couple of weeks?

If so I'd pick them up when or where convenient for you.

Wednesday, [?], 1948

I'm reopening this envelope to thank you for sending on Newton-White's letter. I haven't heard anything of Muriel lately. I find it hard to foresee her future career & can only hope the Lord will look after his own.

Monday, [?], 1948

If this is for the Society of the Deaf report you already sent me a check last week. Thanks anyway.

---

25 Severn Street,
Wednesday, [?], 1949

Thanks for your letter just recived. I'm awfully sorry to hear Mrs Pierce is ill. I hope it may be less serious than it sounds.

Both *Northern Farm* and *MacKenzie River* were so miserably printed the drawings were hardly recognizable. I hope if I can get my housing problems settled to give some thought to the book you mention for 1950. I get lazier & more indifferent all the time for some reason.

Northern Farm is in 3rd printing.

[?], 1950

I meant to call & thank you for the books, both very interesting. I'm only sorry Needler's cover wasn't printed Black 'stead of that rather sick green ink. When choosing ink I always say, any colour as long as it's Black.

It's a good essay though don't you think?

I hope you are both progressing favourably.

Thornhill,
August 16, 1950

Apparently I wasn't paid for the MacKenzie bookplate. I hope you don't intend to pay for it yourself. If so please leave it until I call in.

Thornhill,
June 17, 1951

Frank tells me you are thinking of binding those books in hard covers. I feel myself that it's not worth while. My idea would be to unload as many of this printing as possible & then I may reprint it better. It certainly should not sell for more than $1.50.

The present printing doesn't do justice to the drawings but I hope to correct this later. Better just stitch them up in paper as intended.

Hope to see you again shortly.

Thornhill,
Thursday, [?], 1951

I have the estimate for the *Woods & Fields* book.

For 500 copies paper covers, collated and stitched $242.00 plus tax or about 50¢ each. 1 M should be considerably less per copy. Just rec'd my royalties for the Group of 7; $12.12. It's now out of print. So far I never had anything for the Woodchuck book of cuts. Wonder how it is. I'll call soon as I have the introductory note etc. & hope you both have a good Easter.

Might put in some drawings from *Village of Viger* if the Ryerson Press hasn't lost them.

Thornhill,
Friday, [?], 1951

Thanks for your letter & check. I'm sorry to have given you this extra trouble.

I have about 35 pages all ready mounted up & about 10 more to do. There won't be a great deal of retrospection as it's impossible to get the originals & proofs are little use. Plates of *Viger* book won't help either; for this process drawings are needed. However, I have plenty & may have to eliminate some as it is.

Thornhill,
Thursday, [?], 1951

I haven't been able to find the zinc for *Happy Thought* so if you send me the greeting copy I'll letter it offset. This should be economical as I can put it on the same plate with another Xmas card & run them at one time.

Also please tell me how many.

Please don't delay as it will soon be hard to get things done.

Thornhill, Friday, [?], 1951

I think the paper of your bookplate is too rough for the little label. I'd suggest Plainfield Offset, Ivory 100 M; same as above label. I would have even less margin, about like this.

Thornhill,
Sat Evening, [?], 1952

I've been thinking over your proposed Xmas card & it seems to me it would be better to draw it by hand with an initial.

Perhaps you will give me the copy when it's ready & I'll make a layout. You will run into a lot of bother setting it in type.

Thornhill,
Tuesday, [?], 1952

Thanks for yours of Sunday. I've been intending to call at your office but it's hard getting around in Toronto & I thought you would be busy getting ready for February 14.

I thought better not have a personal prospectus for Bice's show so I submitted a few words on line drawing in general but perhaps they proved unnecessary. He was pleased with the drawings. He exhibited some from Dartmouth which should give enough for a show.

It's hard to get people to look at drawings.

I hope to call at your office before you leave.

Thornhill,
Tuesday, [?], 1952

I heard you were asking about the Group of 7. It's in the press & should be ready any day. A good many difficulties arose. Some photos weren't available & others wouldn't reproduce, among them 'The Elements.'

I hope your summer has been beneficial.

[?], 1953

The best things I can think of for that French book would be my father's 'Lonely North' and perhaps Comfort's 'Barns and Ploughshare.'
They should make a striking pair *if reproduced well.*

I have photo of 'Lonely North' & could get the other from Comfort.

Thornhill,
[January 10, 1954]

I 've put off thanking you for the Canada book, meaning to call at your office.
I appreciate your sending it & hope things are as well as possible with you.

Thornhill,
[March 4, 1954]

I thought I'd let you know that at last I've gone over those drawings for Queens. There will be 12 mounts with a total of 58 drawings. One is still in Paul Duval's possession & 3 were borrowed by the Willistead Gallery in Windsor.
If your Bindery makes a case the inside measurements should be 20½ x 16½ x 3″. I guess it should consist of a cover & slip case. If you wish I can get one made. I would stick the list of contents inside the cover. Should be some plain brown or gray stock. Sorry to bother you with this but if you approve I can go on & clear it up.

Thoreau MacDonald

Thornhill March 4
[1954]

Dear L. P.

I thought I'd let you know that at last I've gone over those drawings for Queens. There will be 12 mounts with a total of 58 drawings. One is still in Paul Duval's possession & 3 were borrowed by the Willistead Gallery in Windsor.

If your Bindery makes a case the inside measurements should be ~~21 x 17 x~~ $20\frac{1}{2}$ X $16\frac{1}{2}$ X $2\frac{1}{2}$ " I guess it should consist of a cover & slip case If you wish I can get one made. I would stick the list of contents inside the cover, Should be some plain brown or gray stock.

Sorry to bother you with this but if you approve I can go on & clean it up,

Thoreau

172

[?], 1954

If it's not too late & you're agreeable I think we should take out that Black Spruce of mine & substitute my father's Beaver Dam. It's far better & more suitable. The spruce picture doesn't photograph well & seems to me the old Beaver Dam should be in.

I phoned Charles Comfort & he promised to send his material to your office. He may forget.

I enclose print of Beaver Dam. I'd like to get all photos again when you're through.

[?], 1954

When I started to draw the additional 3 lines the proof looked so bad I redrew the whole thing. It's slightly improved so if convenient please make a new cut. This will be better than locking in the last lines.

After cut is made the drawing should go to Mr Mitchell for use on offset cover.

I hope to see you at Thornhill soon.

Thornhill, Friday, [?], 1955

I guess I'll have to decline with thanks the invitation to your home on Sunday. Probably you won't be surprised, but I'll call around there sometime before long. I have written out for the 4th time a note on J.E.H. MacD. Not more than 1100 words & can't seem to make it longer.

The German proofs I felt were not quite good enough, just missed the feel of the original. I showed it to Casson & he thought a little more work on the plates might bring it to standard.

[?], 1955

Here's a layout for the greeting. It's the same size but seems to fit better horizontally. I thought the opening caps might be in green or anyway the first line. If you approve I'll make a drawing & have it done by offset. Call at Thornhill anytime you are near or have spare time.

Thornhill, Tuesday, [?], 1955

As requested I'm enclosing a bill, the work didn't take long.

We have just had rather an upset in the family. Yesterday my mother got hit with a car; got broken ribs & pelvis. However she seems fairly cheerful & has little pain if she keeps still. Will be in hospital for some weeks. Dr hopes a cast won't be necessary. Duval called here & would like to push on my father's proposed book. Says he could sell enough signed copies to pay for it. He may speak with you about it sometime. I have no such hopes.

I hope your teeth won't be too bothersome.

Saturday, [?], 1956

Rec'd this after writing. After careful & solitary comparison of proof & original it seems to leave quite a lot to be desired. Maybe as Casson said further work on plates would do it. Maybe it's the absence of black plate. I'm not experienced but can see it misses the feel of original. Can't say I'm entirely satisfied. I think there's quite a lot lost in the proof, some depth & richness. Needs further work seems to me. Note rather crude blues & yellows on far shore, the proof misses the depth & harmony of original.

[November 23, 1956]

This is a sample copy of that booklet we spoke of when you were at Thornhill. I haven't got exact costs yet but hope they'll not be more than 35¢ each, perhaps less. Envelopes were not included. If you can use any I would send them.

Hope you feel well.

If you prefer the drawing just let me know what lettering you want.

Thornhill, [July 12, 1957]

I've a note from Newton-White in which he says he would rather not cut his mss & anyhow couldn't do anything on it before next winter.

If you feel it's not suitable he suggests sending it to Faber & Faber.

Perhaps sometime before long you'll let me know what you think & I'll pick it up at your office.

Thanks & best regards.

Thornhill, [October 9, 1957]

I'm rather uncertain about proceeding with the Newton-White drawings as he feels a little doubtful of the book being finally published, at least in its original form. I think it would be a pity to cut the criticisms of Government, Pulp & Paper & so on. I feel those sharp points are essential to the Porcupine. It seems to me such things badly need saying & that all the bad news in the book can't be over emphasized. Anyway I thought best to ask you before going further. It's an awful effort to start.

I hope you have been well & will call at Thornhill before long.

Sunday, [?], 1958

I wanted to thank you for the book of *Early Canada* pictures. It's a very luxurious present. I'm returning these reviews of E.N.W.'s book. Anyway they acknowledge its importance.

I've heard no more about the St Lawrence book. I'm a poor one to illustrate it as I know hardly anything about the river.

I hope you have a good year & write a book.

[?], 1958

I'm so sorry we were away when you came Saturday. We had gone to the hospital to see Julia B. She took a turn for the worse about 10 days ago & has been in Branson Hospital for a week. Her Dr says he's pleased with her progress now.

Please come again when you can. When we go to the hospital we usually leave about 2 PM. Perhaps you also might go, though hospital calls aren't always fun. But Branson is very nice.

Thanks for coming & hoping to see you before long.

Thornhill, [July 17, 1958]

Thanks for copies of the label & cheque enclosed. You already sent me one for the bookplate but perhaps this is for the lettering to go with C.L. Burton's copy of Chaucer. If so we are now all square.

The printer has returned me the drawing for your bookplate & I'll keep it for you or until I'm near your office. I hope you'll return rested.

Decided to send you the bookplate design now in case you want to send it to Queens.

Thornhill, Ontario,
November 18, 1958

Christmas Card Design = $12.00
    Thanks for note of 16th November. We will look for you Sunday afternoon the 23rd. I've enclosed a rough layout for the proposed St Lawrence book. I thought to make some half page drawings or even 2 page spreads, then some fillers for any available space. I don't know the title yet.

[December 3, 1958]

Thank you for the Canadian Field Naturalist & review of N.W.'s book. It's a careful review but prejudiced I think. Perhaps by the reviewer's official position. To me everything seems far worse & more hopeless than N.W. makes out.
    I enclose a couple of extracts from a letter I got from a young forester friend on the same subject. He's an interesting writer & a good forester. Hoping to see you soon.

I had a copy of Jackson's book given to me.

[?], 1959

Re: Memories of Tom Thomson

Very few records by people who knew him personally & all out of print. These are by —

J.E.H. MacD., Dr MacCallum, A.H. Robson, T. MacD. Why not reprint these accounts* in one pamphlet with one or two portraits, a colour reproduction, photos or drawings of T's shack, cairn, etc. All this material is available free & the finished record would be useful to future students, if any appear.

Dr MacC	4000
Robson	1800
J MacD	1200
T MacD	1000
	8000 words

* other material if available but firsthand only, no hearsay

Tuesday, [?], 1959

Thanks for returning paper & thanks again for your interest in the case.

I'll bring down that little sketch of 'The Elements' sky. You can keep it as long as you wish. My mother asked me to say she's glad the picture will be in Toronto. Let me know if they put on that party & I'll make an effort to attend.

Please come to Thornhill any day you have time.

Tuesday, [?], 1959

I hope you're feeling better. I have made very poor progress on the Locke nature book, partly pressure of family work & partly old age. Please let me know the absolute deadline for delivery of drawings.

[?], 1959

I've looked over these projects & certainly would advise against the St Lawrence poems.

The nature essays would be very easy to work with but I don't know about sales. I think the format of the book should be a little different, probably like Scott's *Village of Viger*. I don't know if you plan a drawing for each essay. There are 32. Perhaps some could be omitted but I could make them without too much expense. Altogether I'd be for trying it.

I enclose a layout for the *Hearing* magazine. It might be some improvement but probably it's futile to try to do much with it. Such publications seemed doomed to look terrible.

Lastly, I thought over the material for that proposed Tom Thomson booklet. It seems rather trivial for the trouble involved & I think I'd vote against going further with it. Perhaps it might go in *The Canadian Forum* or some such paper.

Perhaps you'll let me know about the nature notes & *The Hearing Eye* & I'll get going on them. Better finish up the latter before you leave.

Sunday, [?], 1959

I forgot after all to return this to you yesterday.

I was sorry you & Mr McNaught didn't stay longer, we might have got some tea & we still have your records. Please come again next week or first opportunity. I'm hoping to make better progress with those little drawings & will soon send a layout for title page & jacket.

Text, binding & paper may as well follow *Village of Viger*.

Thornhill, Sunday, [?], 1959

Thanks for your letter. I didn't have much enthusiasm for that Thomson project but while you're away I'll try to get it ready even if we never use it.

I find no mention of those nature essays. If you make a decision on them before leaving perhaps Miss Daley would let me know & I could work on the drawings through the last of the winter.

I hope you have a good journey & make lots of photos.

Thornhill, [July 31, 1959]

I received the cheque with thanks. I hardly feel I should accept it. If you think we should have included another 2 or 3 institutions for groups of drawings perhaps I could make up a couple more sets.

Come to Thornhill when you have time.

[October 27, 1959]

I don't know Tom Thomson's address other than 25 Severn Street.

McMichael would know or could find out from Tom's sister who's a friend of theirs. M. & his wife are in New York where they are opening a branch office. This is probably why you didn't hear from them. Last time I saw him he said he hoped to get you to Kleinburg to see his new basement picture room. If you can wait a week or so for Tom's addresses I think they can be found.

He once boarded on Gould Street, I think.

Thornhill, Friday, [?], 1960

Thanks for the copy of *Canadian Nation*. It looks well & I feel the content is good if rather more hopeful than my own view. I can't imagine what Canada's future will be. It seems as if only poor countries can amount to much.

I meant to write sooner but the ice storms caused such damage we had to chop our way out. It will be a long time before things are cleared up & we lost a great many trees.

Please come to Thornhill any time.

Thornhill, [January 6, 1960]

I forgot about the jacket for *Canadian Nation* until your office sent an engraver's proof. It looks OK & I hope your pressman will get a nice sharp impression. We are busy as we lost a great many trees in the ice storm. Only one really big, 44″ diameter & 95′ high. Many smaller trees bent to the ground & broke off. But we should soon get more order out of the wreck.

Thornhill, [September 21, 1960]

The date you mention Saturday, October 1 will be all right, D.V. Any time of day. The walls are light so maybe a screen will not be necessary. Meantime I will try to think of some suitable drawing for Christmas. We are always glad for you to come any time.

Thornhill, [August 21, 1961]

Thanks for your kind letter. I'll take up the subjects in their order. I have modified the lettering for your Xmas card & will proceed with printing. I'm enclosing a bill for this & the wash drawing.

I have estimates for Mr Locke's books. They are higher than I hoped but are outside estimates with a chance of saving here & there. The figures are between $520-$585.00. It's a small run & an additional 100 copies wouldn't make much difference. It will make about 42 pages.

That is a very kind offer on the reproductions. I haven't given up the idea but there's some hope of getting a publisher & avoiding some or most of the expense. *I really appreciate that kind offer.*

Please let me know about Mr Locke's book. I can't think of a much cheaper way. To set it up in type & make cuts would be far more.

[?]

Re: The Story of the Club

Hope the Committee will OK this. It may be necessary to send out for the type as I don't think they would accept old 21E.

This other cut should have J.M.'s name removed & the enclosed title set up under it.

[?]

Re: *In The Village of Viger*

Stories should have gone straight ahead as it's quite correct to start them on the verso page. Plenty of precedent for this & avoids irritating holes in the book. Might make little vignettes for the blanks.

Jacket - Black on Mayfair
General layout as *Peggy's Cove* jacket
Please let me see a proof.

Thornhill, Tuesday, [?]

I should have thanked you for sending the photos but thought I might have seen you.

I've been thinking you had better not lend me that mountain sketch. Something might happen to it & I have plenty of them. I often worry about them in this old wooden house.

I hope Dr Stock was satisfied with his cards. He ordered 600.

Thursday, [?]

Thanks for your note & appreciation of Locke's book. I hope it turns out well. They will try hard anyhow.

I had a visit from Mr & Mrs Gerald Stevens. I expect you saw them also. I do hope you're feeling better & will soon be able to get to Thornhill.

Thornhill, Saturday, [?]

I have the type for Mr Locke's book ready to stick together. In this process I can't give him proofs as there's only the one copy. I'd better paste it up with drawings & then you can both look it over. Corrections can be inserted without too much trouble.

It's been a headache as the type isn't size AS, but set big & then

183

reduced. Makes it hard to fit in drawings.

We hope you feel better & can soon come to Thornhill.

CHAPTER VIII

Letters to Norman Kent

25 Severn Street,
Toronto, December 24, 1942

Many thanks for your kind letter which came today, also the history of the Bank, a fine production which I'm very glad to have. It's a beautiful job.

NORMAN KENT is described by Margaret Edison as 'another expert in the field of design and illustration' with whom an exchange of ideas with Thoreau resulted 'in Kent's major article in the January 1946 issue of *American Artist: "Thoreau MacDonald, Canadian Illustrator."* '

I would have been glad to hear from you when you were here & hope if you return you will call me, at night you could get me at Thornhill 101, as I don't live in Toronto. About the books you mention, I haven't seen copies of *Old Province Tales* nor *The Chopping Bee* for many years & suppose they're out of print. You certainly won't miss much as my work on them was pretty feeble. If I had a copy of *Early Woodcuts* I would gladly send it to you but so far haven't located one. It was only a little booklet about 4 x 3″ containing a few lino cuts. I will ask Dents if they have any *Canadian Forum Reproductions* left. Of the books listed by Mr Hunter only about 3 are well done. *J.E.H. MacDonald, West by East,* & *Maria Chapdelaine.* I have some of the Woodchuck booklets but haven't done anything new since the war. Old copies of *The Canadian Forum* are scarce & I believe there are only 2 complete files in Canada.

This doesn't sound very helpful but if I can do anything further I will be very pleased. Thank you again for writing & for the book which already has been much admired.

[?], 1943

My thanks, Mr Kent, for the beautiful prints. I like the watercolours too, especially 'The Derelict.'

I'm asking Ryerson Press to forward you Hunter's *J.E.H. MacDonald. West By East* is out of print they tell me. *Maria Chapdelain* is published by Macmillan at $2.50. I enclose all Woodchuck Press material.

I certainly appreciate the prints.

---

25 Severn Street,
Toronto, March 14, [?]

I'm sending today what examples I've been able to gather, rather a ragtag lot I'm afraid. Some drawings are borrowed so I'll have to ask you to return them if it's not too much bother. Some good stuff I was unable to get hold of as it belongs to Hunter, now in Florida.

The books from which drawings were taken —
Maria Chapdelaine by Louis Hémon, Macmillan, 1938
Mountain Cloud by Marius Barbeau, Caxton-Macmillan, 1944
In the Village of Viger by Duncan Campbell Scott, Ryerson, 1945

I hope you'll find something suitable in these & with thanks for your interest.

---

25 Severn Street,
Toronto 5, November 1, [?]

Many thanks for your letter. Of course you're right re offset printing as compared with any relief process. My only reason for using offset was ECONOMY, a great consideration in such ventures.

I'm glad to hear of Wilson's new illustrations & will hope eventually to see them in Toronto. The *American Artist* will certainly be appreciated though I've felt a bit shy at receiving it *gratis*. I had thought to subscribe before now, but, as I said, economy is very essential at present. I expect to buy a new tractor this spring. I would be glad if you could think of anything I could do for the magazine. I'm not in very close touch with the art world but would do my best.

6

The Trinity University
REVIEW

VOLUME LVIII   NUMBER FOUR

The TRINITY UNIVERSITY REVIEW

[?]

The parcel of *American Artists* arrived today & I look forward to looking at them. Many, many thanks.

As you see above we're still at winter work in subzero weather with lots of snow.

---

25 Severn Street,
Toronto, April 23, [?]

I just received another number of the *American Artist*. I hadn't realized when I wrote before that I was to receive it regularly so I send additional thanks.

I hope you get the drawings I sent without trouble. I'm enclosing a couple of extra proofs if they're any use. One is a book-jacket for the Ryerson Press, Toronto, the other one for my hawks & owls set.

Thornhill, Ontario,
[March 24, 1947]

Believe me I sympathize with you in losing your father. Though it's 15 years since my own died I've not forgotten my feelings then & still think of him every day. A father means a lot to a man at any time of life. So I found it & I expect you have too.

About the Pulp & Paper reproductions. The size is 20 x 27″ with a ¼″ margin around the print. Some of them were first rate things I thought. The last I heard from the head office the demand had been so heavy they were unable to send out more copies. It's now proposed to publish them in some sort of book form but whether they'll be in colour I don't know. If you like I can forward your enquiry. . . .

I keep grubbing away & hardly know what goes on in the Art World here. Jackson has gone on his annual sketching trip to Quebec.

I was glad to see your article on Norman Price, an old friend of my folks & a great chap. Many thanks again for the magazine.

---

25 Severn Street,
Toronto 5, May 10, [?]

I'm certainly surprised & sorry to hear of your leaving the *American Artist*. I've often thought & heard others say how it's improved since you went there.

I hope to hear you have something as good or better before long. Publishing & bookselling are pretty quiet here. I've done very little in that line lately but have kept busy somehow. *Of course everything is on a very small scale here so that I wonder how Canadian publishers stay in business.* I guess you often think of your father. I remember for a long time after I lost mine how I dreamt about him every night. Presonally I often think fathers are more of a friend than a man's mother but of course every family's different.

A.Y. Jackson is down to the U.S. just now. Took a trip to Washington. *I'm no traveller myself, being like a grouchy old Indian on the reservation: I look out at civilization but stay home.*

Please let me hear when you get settled.

Thornhill, Ontario
March 22, [?]

Many thanks for the dandy catalog. It's an example of how it should be done.

I heard no more about your prints you were going to send. I have done very little art work this winter, more manual labour.

I hope your studio is prosperous.

Thornhill, [June 25, 1952]

I'm glad to hear of your new job on *True*. It should be mighty interesting. I buy it now & then & will more often now & see if I detect your influence.

Thornhill, Ontario,
[December 18, 1951]

I have several copies of *Woods & Fields* & will be glad to send you one. I thought of it before but as I wasn't satisfied with the printing didn't sent it. Some drawings are pretty badly reproduced & I know you don't like offset.

About *Canadian Art.* I very seldom see it & had the idea (perhaps mistaken) that it wasn't very keen on more traditional workers like us.

I'm a poor hand at writing anything on art but would gladly sound out the editor on the idea of reproducing your cuts. If he doesn't take to it we might try *Toronto Saturday Night* where I know the art editor slightly. *I'm out of touch with all the art world now except for occasional commercial work.* I haven't seen *American Artist* for years & didn't know they reviewed the drawings. I've become a real hill-billy.

Thornhill, Sunday, [?], 1954

I don't think I ever thanked you for your Christmas card. I still have it stuck up for I was always fond of those boats.

I didn't hear from your friend but am afraid he may have phoned when none were at home. I'm away from the house much of the time, do less art work than formerly.

I often get *True* & was glad to see those things of Remington's, many of whose things I had in my room when I was young. Used to cut them out of Colliers.

I hope all is well with you. . . .

Thornhill, Ontario,
[Christmas eve, 1958]

I just received your fine card so will answer it right away. Last I heard from you your wife wasn't well & I see you've had a hectic year at home so perhaps she isn't yet better. I'm glad your work at the magazine goes well. I buy it occasionally & get a lot from it. As to my own work, I've done nothing important. I worked last winter with an old friend up north making a book on forest management. It came out in August but naturally sells very poorly. Otherwise only trifling things. Sometimes I make a try at real art but don't show it as anything realistic is out of date here. Do you ever see the paper *Canadian Art?* If not I could send you one & you'd see how things are going in these parts. I hope your work continues rewarding & that you & your family will be happy as well.

Thornhill, [January 8, 1960]

I've been intending to write you ever since Christmas to thank you for the woodcut & now your letter & calendar have come. I had no card worth sending so thought to send a letter.

At Christmas we had a very severe ice storm, power & phone lines & trees all brought don. We have many hundreds of trees, some very big so I had lots of work. I'm really glad to hear of your activity but the *American Artist* is hard to find in Toronto so I've not kept up with its progress very well. You mention some lino cuts of mine. This afternoon I hunted for proofs but found none as they must have been made 30 years ago. I still make an occasional drawing for that same magazine. I only illustrated two books in '59, one technical, on forestry etc., the other nature stuff. This was miserably produced so didn't send it. But if you wish I can do so. I've not printed anything on my own for several years. I think the last was H.D. Thoreau's *Succession of Forest Trees* which I believe I sent you. A Montreal litho firm is making a calendar reproducing some of my father's sketches. They're not my own choice but are beautifully reproduced so I've asked them to send you one.

I also have made some attempts at small oil sketches (trying to learn something of that technique) of animals, moose, foxes & birds. But nearly all my work has been very common place, just lettering, type layouts & so on. Many of the men I worked with have retired lately & I'm beginning to feel like the Last Leaf. I had better hurry up & get something worthwhile done.

Thanks again for all the things sent & especially your letter. Best wishes & regards.

Thornhill, Ontario,
[January 27, 1960]

Many thanks for your letter & calendar. I appreciate them. I look
forward to seeing the magazine with your article & repros.

I haven't seen Jackson for a long time as he now lives near
Ottawa. He's very active still.

I asked the Montreal Litho Co. to send you their calendar
with six offset prints of my father's rough sketches. Let me know if
you didn't get them. Last year they did Tom Thomson's & they
were fine reproductions. About that *Black Spruce* picture, I
phoned the art director responsible, Mr A.J. Casson. . . . The
Black Spruce was one of a set of six by different men.

Thornhill, [February 22, 1960]

I'm sending the Thomson prints from last year's Montreal Litho.
calendar.

Mr Pidduck, their advertising manager is very careful & atten-
tive & I think you'll hear from him eventually. Anyhow, I don't
need this set.

A friend of ours, Robt. McMichael, has lately opened an
office in N.Y.C. He's keen on Group of 7 work & has many fine
examples. He & his wife are building a collection to leave to the
country. He might phone you some day.

Thornhill, Ontario,
March 6, [?]

Thanks for sending me the two magazines. We all like your account of the old Group of 7. As you say the repos. were very disappointing; ordinary halftones would look better.

McMichael says he would like to call you some day soon. He's a young business man making a collection of Group of 7 and Tom Thomson. Knows a lot about them.

May, [?], 1961

Many thanks for the beautifully made note on Woodcuts. I appreciate it. With your permission I'll turn it over to the Colgate Collection of printing, Redpath Library of McGill. I enclose a miserable print of an old favourite cut. I had no means of making a better proof.

Box 197, Thornhill, Ontario,
June 11, 1965

Many thanks for your kind letter and the beautiful woodcuts, especially the fine Bentley – Kent House. We have very few as fine in our parts except perhaps at Niagra-on-the-Lake.

We had no unbound sheets left so I enclose another copy of the *House & Barn* booklet. As to selling any, I thought the price would be $2.50. I printed only 125 copies as I didn't expect to sell many. If anyone did wish to get a copy I would send it from above address. DM Press is very small; whole staff consists of a friend, Frank Yamamoto & his wife.

Box 197, Thornhill, Ontario,
July 2, 1965

Thanks for your kind letter of June 29. Don't worry about putting in those drawings. They may come in handy sometime as fillers.

I saw a friend of yours yesterday, R. McMichael, who took me to Kleinburg to see additions to his collection. A pretty fantastic place. You should see it. Chances of me going to N.Y.C. are very remote. I'm in a state of uncertainty as there's likelihood of our place being taken over . . . for an open space. Don't know how it will end. If ever you come to Toronto please call.

Box 197, Thornhill, Ontario,
October 9, 1965

I'll certainly see that you get a catalog of the J.E.H. MacD. show next month. It's compiled by a Miss Nancy Robertson & I think very competently.

I've looked in vain for those old lino cuts that appeared in the *Canadian Forum.* Also the portfolio of drawings printed in 1927. I found & enclose a couple of sheets from this folder. There must be a complete set around Toronto somewhere but it's just as well forgotten. I also enclose a recent drawing of Tom Thomson made for his home town of Owen Sound. They have a little Thomson Memorial Gallery there & we thought these prints might be sold in aid of their gallery fund.

I haven't got much done lately as we have illness in the family but have some things in mind.

I certainly appreciate your writing up that *House & Barn* pamphlet.

November 3, 1965

I certainly appreciate your writing anything on my drawings.

They tell me the catalog for the MacDonald show isn't yet available. It should be very soon as the affair opens November 12. They will see that you receive one. You'll see from this card that we have a really progressive cleaner here.

Box 197, Thornhill, Ontario,
November 26, 1965

I got a copy of *American Artist* today & want to thank you for the generous article you have written. I was really surprised & I hope you know how much I appreciate it.

I hope you got the J.E.H. MacDonald catalog.

Box 197, Thornhill, Ontario,
January 5, 1966

I don't like to bother you with this but I mislaid a letter from your office in which they offer me extra copies of the December issue at 50¢ each. I enclose $3.00 for six if you'll be kind enough to turn it over to the proper dept.

The article certainly stirred up a lot of interest.

Box 197, Thornhill, Ontario
May 29, [?]

You asked me sometme ago what I was doing so I enclose one of some researches into out of date buildings. I didn't send others as they're mostly photos. As I do them on my own they are pretty economical publications.

This one contains one drawing I like on p. 3, our next door neighbour's house.

I'm glad to see *American Artist* retains its standards.

Box 197, Thornhill, Ontario,
October 15, [?]

I don't know that you have much interest in bookplates. I printed this one for a local collector who specializes in Canadian designers.

April 3, [?]

I'm sorry I seem to have no success in bringing over your prints. The chairman of the A. L.C. exhibit committee writes —

'Thanks for having me in mind to introduce Mr Kent's prints to Toronto. However, I'm afraid this would meet considerable difficulty. Canadian customs regulations allow exhibitions released only against 'in bond' arrangements. They require the full value of all the prints. . . . We are fighting this rigidity but so far without result. . . . Regretting my negative answer re Mr Kent's prints. Signed, N. Hornyansky'

I fear I'm a poor representative for you. The man who arranges shows at the University is expected back from the Army this month & I'll speak to him soon as possible. He is Chas. Comfort, a very able Canadian artist whom you may know of.

---

25 Severn Street, Toronto 5,
Tuesday, [?]

It seems ungracious to suggest any change in your generous article but as you plan to make a book & as it will likely be the final word I hope you won't mind.

As I had no contact with artists other than my father in my young days I thought 6 words added to 1st paragraph would make it accurate. I was raised in the country & got no education beyond the *Little Red Schoolhouse,* 5th year. Leave out about Georgian Bay as I never spent summer there. Summers were spent on the hoe handle & spraying potatoes. As I've done no painting for a good many years better leave out reference to it. Hunter was mistaken there. As to Kent's technique I studied all the good work I could find nor had any other instruction. I hope you won't mind these rather niggling suggestions.

An art dealer & gallery owner tells me it's very hard to bring things over the border & so on. Do you think there would be any difficulty? I'll write when I have definite information. Thanks for sending on letters.

---

25 Severn Street, Toronto,
November 5, [?]

Many thanks for proofs & return of drawings. I also appreciate your sending me the *American Artist* & the kind review of the Group of 7 booklet. I often think of trying to revive the old Woodchuck but lately have not felt so good. Please let me know if we can do anything for you over here.

Later:

I overlooked your letter among the drawings so must thank you
again for writing so kindly. It will be OK with the publishers to
reprint drawings. When I last saw Pierce he had not seen your
review but I told him to watch out for it. I thought it more than
just, myself. Mr Standard was kind enough to send me 2 copies of
that lettering catalog. I'm awfully glad to hear of *Print* & will
mention it whenever possible. Too few Canadians are interested in
such things.

    Again thanks for all your kindness.

Thornhill,
November 16, [?]

I saw Pierce at Ryerson Press & he asked me to tell you that your
review of the Canadian Art Series cheered him up more than anything this fall. The series hasn't been a money maker. He had your
review circulated through their plant to show the effort had been
worth while.

    I write this in the country & no pen available.

[?]

Thanks very much for the Genesee Book. It's a beautiful piece of
work. Of the prints I like the frontispiece especially.

[?]

I'm sorry I've lost your home address. You see by this what I'm
reduced to, printing through a bit of waxed paper with a stamp
pad. I hope you keep well & that your wife is feeling better.

[?]

I meant to say how I appreciated your article on Alden Watson. It was fine. I share his ideas to a great extent. Once illustrated *Walden* myself but as no one seemed interested sold the whole works for $25.00.

I hope to see more of Watson's work.

CHAPTER IX

Notes for *Maria Chapdelaine*